KT-140-526

PERGAMON INTERNATIONAL LIBRARY
of Science, Technology, Engineering and Social Studies
The 1000-volume original paperback library in aid of education,
industrial training and the enjoyment of leisure
Publisher: Robert Maxwell, M.C.

THE BRITISH LABOUR PARTY:
A FUNCTIONING PARTICIPATORY DEMOCRACY

THE PERGAMON TEXTBOOK
INSPECTION COPY SERVICE

An inspection copy of any book published in the Pergamon International Library
will gladly be sent to academic staff without obligation for their consideration for
course adoption or recommendation. Copies may be retained for a period of 60
days from receipt and returned if not suitable. When a particular title is adopted or
recommended for adoption for class use and the recommendation results in a sale
of 12 or more copies, the inspection copy may be retained with our compliments.
The Publishers will be pleased to receive suggestions for revised editions and new
titles to be published in this important International Library.

Other Titles of Interest

THE BRITISH LABOUR PARTY:
A FUNCTIONING PARTICIPATORY DEMOCRACY

by

H. B. COLE

PERGAMON PRESS

OXFORD · NEW YORK · TORONTO · SYDNEY
PARIS · FRANKFURT

U. K.	Pergamon Press Ltd., Headington Hill Hall, Oxford OX3 0BW, England
U. S. A.	Pergamon Press Inc., Maxwell House, Fairview Park, Elmsford, New York 10523, U.S.A.
C A N A D A	Pergamon of Canada Ltd., 75 The East Mall, Toronto, Ontario, Canada
A U S T R A L I A	Pergamon Press (Aust.) Pty. Ltd., 19a Boundary Street, Rushcutters Bay, N.S.W. 2011, Australia
F R A N C E	Pergamon Press SARL, 24 rue des Ecoles, 75240 Paris, Cedex 05, France
WEST GERMANY	Pergamon Press GmbH, 6242 Kronberg-Taunus, Pferdstrasse 1, West Germany

First edition 1977

Library of Congress Cataloging in Publication Data

Cole, Harry B.
The British Labour Party: a functioning participatory democracy.

Bibliography: p.
1. Labour Party (Gt. Brit.) I. Title.
JN1129.L33 1977   329.9'41   77—3380
ISBN 0-08-021811-3 Flexi Cover

Printed in Great Britain by Biddles Ltd, Guildford, Surrey

Contents

*Based on *The Social Contract* (1968).
†Based on *Guild Socialism Re-stated* (1920).
‡Based on *Representative Government* (1910).

Preface

"Effective political parties are the crux of democratic government. . . . Their function is to maximise the participation of the people in decision-making at all levels of government. In short they are the mainspring of all the processes of democracy." (Houghton Report, 1976.)

If they are to perform this function they must themselves be 'democratic'. Harry Cole sets out to define the meaning of this much abused term through the study of three radical political philosophers, Rousseau, John Stuart Mill and G. D. H. Cole, and then to see how far the 'inner-party democracy' of the Labour Party comes up to their ideas.

As a former local Party Agent, now a Constituency Party Chairman, he is well qualified by experience to undertake this task. His conclusion is that the Labour Party is "a highly participatory democratic form of elective aristocracy" which needs to introduce certain reforms to overcome the apathy of some of its members. 'Primary' elections to select candidates are perhaps the most important proposal he makes. Recent cases of conflict 'Left' and 'Right' over the endorsement of a number of MPs makes this a topical issue. Arguments about the respective roles of the Parliamentary Labour Party, the National Executive Committee and Conference are perennial in the history of the Movement. This study is a useful contribution to the understanding of the issues involved, based on a genuine attempt to unite theory and practice.

Students of politics – and active practitioners – will find it a helpful addition to the available literature on the subject. It is an example of what can be achieved by a highly motivated adult student, given a little time and opportunity to read, think and reflect on his experience of life.

H. D. HUGHES

26 *November* 1976   Principal, Ruskin College, Oxford

Acknowledgements

I was writing an essay on Rousseau's Social Contract in November 1970 during my first term as a student at Ruskin College, Oxford, when it struck me how closely Rousseau's Republic with its 'General Will' and 'Civil Religion' resembles the structure, constitution and participatory nature of the British Labour Party. I was encouraged by my tutor Paul Brodetsky, and by the Vice-Principal, John D. Hughes, to develop this as my thesis for the Labour Studies Diploma. During my labours on it I was supervised by the Principal Mr. H. D. (Billy) Hughes whose encouragement and pressure drove me through a long arduous labour to the eventual birth of this tiny creation. I thank all three of them and exonerate them from blame for any imperfections in the final issue.

I must also thank the Lady Librarian, Mrs. I. Wagner, at Transport House, Smith Square, for her very patient and courteous pandering to my requirements. Also Reg Underhill, the Labour Party National Agent, and Miss Betty Lockwood, the then Chief Woman Officer and Assistant National Agent, for the massive quantities of material they made available to me concerning the Youth Movement and the Women's Movement respectively, and Geoffrey Foster, Regional Organiser, Southern Region of the Labour Party, for his unstinting help when it was requested.

My grateful thanks also to Bill (Lord) McCarthy for reading the document and for his very constructive criticism and guidance, to Bob Maxwell who also read it and helped me to get the title right and for sticking his neck out in publishing it.

My gratitude to Carole Pateman whose book *Participation and Democratic Theory* (Cambridge U.P., 1970) showed me how to prove my thesis instead of merely asserting it; and to Ralph Berry without whose book, *How to Write a Research Paper* (Pergamon Press, 1966) I would never have mastered the mechanics of producing this document.

And finally to my wife Doreen and my two youngsters for putting up with my irritable presence during the whole of the gestation period.

HARRY B. COLE

Introduction

Books that set out to prove the contemporary relevance of classical political theory are common enough. Books that explain how the Labour Party works — or fails to work — are two-a-penny. What makes this study unusual is that its author applies alternative theories of democracy to the day-to-day working of a party he understands from the inside. What makes it unique is that the task is accomplished with objectivity and affection, in an honest attempt to search out the Party's strengths and weaknesses.

What Harry Cole shows is that the Labour Party is both an instrument for attaining and keeping power *and* an exercise in participative democracy. Virtually all previous writers on the subject (including McKenzie and Milliband) have not been prepared to face this fact or think it through. Consequently they have written longer books, but provided less sure guides to what the party was about.

What Cole argues is that the complex balance between ideology and interest that is the essence of the Labour Party can best be understood by employing a number of concepts first developed by theorists such as Rousseau Cole and Mill. This is a novel idea which I find enlightening and essentially true — especially in the case of Rousseau's notions of 'the lawgiver' and the 'General Will'.

If books really changed how journalists wrote, or academics taught, or the public thought about politics, a whole range of misconceptions would be destroyed by this book's publication. As it is, we can at least say that those who read it without prejudice will no longer be able to complain that the processes of Labour Party democracy are quite beyond their comprehension.

WILLIAM McCARTHY

CHAPTER 1

Introduction

The British Labour Party purports to be a functioning Democracy, but it nowhere precisely defines the concept in relation to itself. It is nevertheless clear to all who are acquainted with the Party, that what is meant, is that the constitution and structural institutions of the Party enables its membership to participate in its work and decision-making processes. The concept, therefore, is one calling for the allowance of more personal involvement of ordinary members in the vital functions of Party government and administration than is usually thought possible or even desirable within a Western Democratic State or its constituent political institutions.

Individual theories of democracy have usually been expounded to relate to the government and administration of the Sovereign Nation State despite the fact that the original use of the term 'democracy' denoted one of the three forms of government in current use in the Greek City States in or around the fifth century B.C. The other two forms were Monarchy and Aristocracy, neither of which require further definition here.

The term 'democracy' relating to the Greek City State was specific. It denoted a government in which all citizens* were able to participate equally in its legislative, executive and administrative functions unless debarred by previous criminal conduct. It gave equal weight to the votes of all citizens regardless of their wealth, position or profession. Its official offices were paid positions of fixed duration, so that no one need be debarred from holding office on grounds of poverty. It also embodied the rights of free speech and freedom of association.

Today the term is ambiguous and virtually all modern governments interpret it in such a way that they can themselves claim to be democratic,

*Citizenship in the Greek City States was usually acquired through inheritance by the male children of citizens. Women, aliens and slaves were not accorded the privileges of citizenship.

1

although none are able to fully satisfy the Ancient Greek criteria. This is either because of the physical limitations to the direct participation of all the citizens, in all aspects of government, due to immense differences between a Greek City State and a modern Nation State, or because freedom of speech and association is curtailed.

Abraham Lincoln defined democracy in his 'Gettysburg Address' as "Government of the people, by the people, for the people", and this definition is generally accepted by the Western Democracies. But, the way in which the concept 'by the people' is implemented through the political party system is being increasingly found wanting – by the people. This is exemplified by the growth of extra-party political organisations which demand to be taken into account when decisions are being made.

> People today . . . have responded to the pressure of events by banding themselves together with others of like mind to campaign vigorously for what they want; and thousands of such pressure groups or action groups have come into existence: Community associations, amenity groups, shop-stewards movements, consumer societies, educational campaigns, organisations to help the old, the homeless, the sick, the poor or underdeveloped societies, militant communal organisations, student power, noise abatement societies, and so on.[1]

This is no new phenomenon. The Anti-Corn Law League and the Chartist movement, working outside the parties, both had considerable effect on political thought and attitudes; while other movements have been absorbed into, or have combined with, one or other of the parties: e.g. Joseph Chamberlain's National Education League, or perhaps the best example might be the infiltration of the Liberal Party by Trade Unionists, and their subsequent repudiation of Liberalism for democratic socialism with the advent of the Labour Party.

Nevertheless, the current plethora of pressure groups each hoping to affect the outcome of some particular issue demonstrates the widespread desire of a significant fraction of the people to participate in the process by which decisions pertaining to at least that issue are made. Furthermore, it testifies to a widely held belief that collective pressure exercised in any field which may possibly influence the ultimate decision, including pressure applied externally and internally to the political parties themselves, may be more effective than attempts to influence decisions by changing or attempting to modify a Party's policy towards the issue through its internal policy-making machinery alone.*

The discernible growth of these beliefs and desires, especially at a time when the Labour Party is trying to identify itself with outside pressure groups through the establishment of Women's Councils, etc., again raises the questions, raised within the Party on many occasions in resolutions to its Annual Conference over the years; is the Party democratic enough? or, does an oligarchic leadership offer a degree of democracy as a sop to retain the membership's services as, a paymaster and/or 'vote getting agency'?[2,3] Additionally the Labour Party's own view of the democracy of its internal government has been classified by authoritative academics as 'wilful self-deception'[4] and, 'a necessary myth'.[5]

In order to look more closely at these questions, I shall examine those Labour Party structures which comprise the Individual and affiliated members and which determine the manner and extent to which members can participate in the activities and decision-making processes of the various bodies to which they may belong within the Party, including Constituency Labour Party Branches, Women's sections and committees, Young Socialist branches and committees, etc., at local, regional and national level as appropriate, in relation to specific theories of democracy.

As I have already pointed out theories of democracy based on the Western Liberal Democracies would be inappropriate for this purpose.† Any theory which admits validity to the Burkean Concept of Representation would render the affirmation of "democracy within the British Labour Party" tautology. What is required is something nearer to Rousseau's — direct democracy — but as

> Michels proved conclusively and with finality, that, for technical and psychological reasons, democracy as he understood it — Rousseau's direct democracy — is impossible to achieve in any large or complex organisation or society[6] ‡

*This technique was employed very effectively by the Campaign for Nuclear Disarmament which, while being a non-political, extra-party organisation, was able to recruit a very large number of Labour Party members and made a deep public impression nationally and internationally during the early 1960s.

†See page 1, paragraph 1.

‡This is a reference to Robert Michels' book *Political Parties*.

my sights must be set somewhat lower than this.

Carole Pateman in her book *Participation and Democratic Theory (1970)* has analysed the democratic theories of J. J. Rousseau, J. S. Mill and G. D. H. Cole to establish a theory of participatory democracy which is based on the psychological impact which active membership of participatory social institutions has on the human personality. The stability of the theory rests on the self-sustaining effect of the educative and integrative nature of the participatory process and Mrs. Pateman has shown that the work of each philosopher establishes these qualities and reinforces their establishment by each of the other theorists.[7]

I shall therefore examine the theories of Rousseau, Cole and Mill, and attempt to establish to which of the theories or to what admixture of them the Labour Party's internal structures most nearly conform and whether such conformity is analogous to participatory democracy within the institution examined.

I will then examine some of the complaints, external and internal, which seek to deny or modify the Labour Party's claim to be a functioning participatory democracy.

Finally, I will summarise my findings and make some recommendations to increase participation or make it more effective.

REFERENCES

1. Anthony Wedgwood Benn, *the new politics a socialist reconnaissance*, Fabian Tract 402, p. 9.
2. *The Labour Party Annual Report 1970*, p. 182.
3. Robert T. McKenzie, *British Political Parties* (1964), p. 636.
4. *Ibid.*, p. 626.
5. W. J. W. MacKenzie, "Mr. McKenzie on the British Parties", *Political Studies*, Vol. 3 (1955), p. 157.
6. Peter V. Medding, "Power in Political Parties", *Political Studies*, No. 18, p. 2.
7. Carole Pateman, *Participation and Democratic Theory* (1970), Chap. 11, p. 22.

CHAPTER 2

The Democratic Theories of Three Advocates

(a) J. J. ROUSSEAU, a theory of maximum participation,
(b) G. D. H. COLE, participation and multiple representation,
(c) J. S. MILL, participation and representation.

Each of these philosophers erected his particular model within the parameters of the Nation State and each believed that the maximum involvement of the people of his polity in all its affairs would render his proposals 'ideal'. Each of them started from a different standpoint and offered a different prognosis.

(a) J. J. Rousseau

The pessimistic Rousseau wished to start with a society of comparative equals, accepting a constitution and body of laws comprising its own General Will, from the hands of an impartial 'Lawgiver'.[1] A society in which all the citizens would be allowed, would be prepared and would wish to take part in every aspect of its government and in which the people would be sovereign. Sovereignty, after the acceptance of the General Will, comprising the ability to legislate on all matters affecting the General Will.[2]

THE 'GENERAL WILL'

This was not just the will of the majority at any given time, it was the collective acceptance by the whole people of a binding set of general rules, ideas and procedures for the government of everyone in the interests of all. Thus as a citizen accepting the 'constitution' I voted for everything that was in my own best interest, and, for the most part, that which was in my best interest coincided with that which was in the best interest of all. This is because some of the fractional selfish interests of all, excepting the tiny minority whose selfish interests coincided with mine, were suppressed on my behalf. Therefore when some of my own selfish interests were subsequently suppressed, I was merely surrendering the freedom to pursue those of my selfish interests whose pursuit would have been to the detriment of my fellow citizens, for the greater freedom brought about by the combined sacrifice by every other person of his right to promote those of his interests which could only be achieved to the detriment of myself or others.

> . . . since each man gives himself to all, he gives himself to no one; and since there is no associate over whom he does not gain the same rights as others gain over him, each man recovers the equivalent of everything he loses, and in the bargain he acquires more power to preserve what he has.[3]

The 'General Will' therefore is my own 'true will' because I value that greater freedom, the freedom from fear and from the exercise of eternal vigilance against all others, more than the lesser freedom to take from anyone, anything or everything he holds if I am able, and to hold whatever I possess against all others as long as I can.

> Those who are associated in it take collectively the name of a *people*, and call themselves individually *citizens*, in so far as they share in the sovereign power, and *subjects*, in so far as they put themselves under the laws of the state.[4]

Every citizen therefore had equal rights and equal responsibilities under the 'general will/constitution' so it became the duty and the privilege of the people to elect a government which would administer the General Will.

DEMOCRACY

In a 'true democracy' the government would be elected by lot.

> . . . for, where all men were equal in character and talent as well as in principles and fortune, it would hardly matter who was chosen.[5]

But, because of size and the complexities of issues in anything larger than a Greek City State or a Swiss canton, and because of the cupidity of human beings, Rousseau did not believe that 'true democracy' was attainable.

In the strict sense of the term, there has never been a true democracy, and there never will be... If there were a nation of Gods, it would govern itself democratically. A government so perfect is not suited to men.[6] *

But Rousseau uses the term 'democracy' in two ways; in his 'ideal' sense of 'true democracy', and, in a more practical way when he says,

... in general democratic government suits small states, aristocratic government suits states of intermediate size and monarchy suits large states... but how are we to calculate the multitude of particular circumstances which may offer exceptions to the rule.

having already said,

... the three forms of government may be combined to yield a multitude of mixed forms, each of which it can multiply by the three simple forms.[7]

A democratic polity may therefore choose an elective aristocracy to form its government providing it is elected by the sovereign and providing that there is a high enough degree of participation by the people, if the procedures regulating the elections laid down in the constitution is followed. Indeed, an elective aristocracy was the best of all governments for all but primitive peoples.[8]

Rousseau nevertheless laid down the criteria which must pertain for the initiation of 'pure democracy', i.e.

... a very small state, where the people may be readily assembled and where each citizen may readily know all the others... a great simplicity of manners and morals,... a large measure of equality in social rank and fortune,... little or no luxury[9]

And, moving always further away from the 'ideal', he went on to provide the criteria for the initiation of weaker forms of democratic polity: as states become larger and more complex to administer; as the people become richer, more attuned to self-interest and therefore less active in the affairs of state; or, as governments use their power to further their own rather than the GENERAL Will; so will democracy be more difficult to initiate or maintain[10] until inevitably it must deteriorate and die. A good

*Rousseau's Republic as outlined in the Social Contract was not therefore a 'true democracy' because its citizens could not participate directly in all of its governmental functions; but, he used the term democracy, also to define popular control of governments.

constitution might prolong its life, but even that could not save it. It was doomed to be converted to either aristocracy or Ochlocracy.[11] *

THE CIVIL RELIGION

Rousseau maintains that all states are based on a religion and that all states subject to a General Will should be based on a civil religion, the articles of which would not in the main be religious dogmas but sentiments of sociability, without which it would be impossible to be either a good citizen or a loyal subject. The sovereign would be able to banish from the state, anyone who did not believe the articles, as an anti-social being, and anyone who professed to believe them and then acted as if he did not should be put to death.[12] The civil religion therefore was not theology but ideology. In fact Professor Talmon in his book *The Origins of Totalitarian Democracy* believes that Rousseau laid down the framework on which totalitarian democracy was built, i.e. dictatorship resting on popular enthusiasm based on ideology.[13] Rousseau's model contains what might be termed a declining scale for the probability of continuing democratic government and its inevitable degeneration.

(b) G. D. H. Cole, Participation and Multiple Representation

Cole's model is avowedly socialist (Guild Socialism) and is designed within the parameters of a modern industrial Nation State to provide a pattern by which " . . . the broadening and deepening demand of the organised workers for the 'control of Industry' "[14] could be achieved, in order to change some and create other institutions governing the control and decision-making processes which affect his citizen/guildsman. Like Mill, Cole eschews the principle of 'one man one vote', but for very different reasons. Cole's model is built on direct participation and functional representation, his guildsman must have

> . . . free choice of, constant contact with and considerable control over, his representative . . . he should be called upon, not to choose someone to represent him as a man or as a citizen in all the aspects of citizenship, but only

*Mob rule.

to choose someone to represent his point of view in relation to some particular purpose or group of purposes, in other words, some particular *function*. All true and democratic representation is therefore *functional* representation.[15]

Representation by different people, for different purposes, at numerous different levels, both horizontally (at local level) and vertically (regionally and nationally); ". . . man should have as many distinct and separately exercised votes as he has distinct social purposes or principles".[16]

Cole's guildsman represents himself by direct participation, in the affairs of the ward or village in which he resides, in the local unit of his industrial or agricultural guild and in his local consumer co-operative. The Industrial Guilds comprise all the workers by hand and by brain in each industrial grouping, they are democratically self-governing, all levels of management being appointed directly by or with the approval of the managed. And, all actions and decisions concerning every aspect of the working of each concern are taken by, or on behalf of, all the workers by functional representatives who are subject to recall. The guilds themselves are based on the workplace, each local unit is directly represented on its district or regional unit, each region is represented on the National Guild and all National Guilds are represented on the Industrial Guilds Congress which would also receive representatives from local and regional guild councils. The guilds may be organized on two bases: a single industry requiring a large degree of central organisation, mostly primary producers, e.g. coal, electricity, gas, railways, road transport, steel, etc.; or, manufacturing industry or groups of industries, whose organisational needs can often be fully met locally, usually intermediate consumers of primary products, e.g. engineering, textiles, plastics, paper printing, etc. Between the vast complex of guilds, at all levels, will flow an intricate, heterogeneous multicurrent of intercourse, conveying not only the necessary interchange of material, commodities and intelligence essential for commercial efficiency. But also the provision and exchange of information and personnel which will make inter- and intra-guild participation a meaningful exercise for the mutual advancement of democracy and social standards within the polity. Each guild unit at every level would have representation on the appropriate Guild Council and the relevant commune which between them would co-ordinate the commercial and social criteria which would determine the overall control and administration of the social utilisation of industrial resources at that particular level.

The whole membership of each ward or village would be able to participate in all of its functions and in the functions of the Consumer Co-operative which serviced its inhabitants as the distributor of domestic consumer products and as provider of the relevant data necessary for consumer protection.

The general meetings of wards, villages* and consumer co-operatives would be open to all members with equal rights, but the day-to-day running of each may be in the hands of a committee elected at agreed intervals by democratic process. Representatives from the wards would be elected to a Town Council, to Cultural and Health Councils and to a Town Commune, while representatives from consumer co-operatives would be elected to a Town Co-operative Consumer Council.

The Town Council would be responsible for the employment of Civic Guilds dealing with Health, Education and other municipal services; and for a Collective Utilities Council which would provide protection for consumers against the centrally administered and distributed Utility Services, i.e. water, gas, electricity, etc.

All of the Councils – the industrial guilds council, the civic guilds council, the two consumer bodies and the cultural and health councils, together with representatives of the wards – would be represented on the Town Commune, the functions of which would be principally those of co-ordination.

All local councils would provide representatives to their regional equivalents, which in turn would provide representation on the Regional Commune. This would co-ordinate urban and rural organisations as Town and Township Communes would also have direct representation to it. The National Commune (which would replace Parliament in a co-ordinating capacity) would be elected from the National equivalent of the Regional bodies, plus representatives from the Regional Communes.

Cole's polity gives his guildsman/citizen/consumer the ability to affect the processes which govern the conduct and quality of his life by

---

*Villages have the same structure and abilities as wards except that their representatives serve on Rural Township instead of Town Councils and Communes, so from this point references to wards should be taken to include villages.

establishing effective decision-making power at a level which makes it possible for him to influence it directly, in his own industrial unit, through the ward in which he lives or through his consumer co-operative. This is made easier by conditions of financial and educational equality. Pay, ideally, although it may be allocated by the guild in which the worker has membership, would not be in respect of work done, but would be based on social considerations.[17] Neither unemployment nor full-time education would therefore create a financial problem for him. Furthermore, the quantity of information which would have to be made available in self-governing enterprises and services would have a cumulative effect, would stimulate discussion on practical management problems and functional alternatives and would interest workers in trying to promote the practical application of their own ideas, leading to the deeper involvement of increased participation because of its combined educational and integrative effects. Dirty and unpleasant work would be rewarded by shorter hours, thereby making it more attractive to workers whose extra-occupational interests were more demanding of their leisure time.[18]

Cole provides a multiplicity of avenues both vertical and horizontal by which individuals may seek; to promote the separate representation of their several distinct views in the numerous areas of decision which affects their lives; or, themselves to represent others.

(c) J. S. Mill, Participation and Representation

John Stuart Mill believing that democracy was inevitable, and within limits desirable, attempted to construct a suitably practical and practicable model based on the social situation as he found it. This meant that from the start his construction must encompass a situation of great inequality of wealth, education, social status, etc., within a large Nation State which was experiencing the political turbulance accompanying increasing industrialisation. Mill did not believe as Rousseau did, that comparative equality was necessary for the establishment of democracy. But he was deeply committed to the preservation of individual negative freedoms. Any extension of the popular control of government therefore gave rise to two great fears which, if they were not to be realised, created a formidable problem. The two fears were: (1) The danger of an increase in the activity and therefore the power, of government. (2) The danger of 'class legislation', which he called "one of the greatest dangers, . . . of democracy".[19]

His problem, therefore, was to devise a system of government which would gain the allegiance of the numerical majority (the labouring classes), without giving them the ability to control the government.

GOVERNMENT INTERFERENCE

To Mill government action especially at local level, unless it was purely advisory, to help people to help themselves, was unwarranted interference. Such interference had to be restricted because of ". . . the great evil of adding unnecessarily to its (government's) power".[20] People should therefore be allowed to govern themselves at local level, not only in order to restrict this interference and ensure that the government did not become too powerful, but also for the educational effect that this would have on participants.

> In many cases, though, individuals may not do the particular thing so well, on the average, as the officers of government, it is nevertheless desirable that it should be done by them, rather than by the government, as a means to their own mental education – a mode of strengthening their active faculties, exercising their judgement, and giving them a familiar knowledge of the subjects with which they are thus left to deal.[21]

CLASS LEGISLATION

Mill was contemptuous of the Chartist call for Manhood Suffrage. He thought the franchise should be extended to all adults, both male and female. But he was deeply afraid of the possibility of class legislation, ". . . the sinister interest of the holders of power", that the numerical majority comprising the labouring class might, through lack of intelligence and tuition, having gained control of the government, legislate in their own short-term interest against savings and against inheritance, ". . . in opposition to justice, at the expense of all other classes and of prosperity".[22]

He felt that a democratic system of government should contain some mechanism for balancing the representation of the classes to avoid a majority dictatorship. He approved of the 'temporary' witholding of the franchise under a system of elementary educational qualification, and from those who had drawn poor relief within five years.

He advocated the introduction of proportional representation so that minorities would not be entirely excluded, and he hoped that the female electors would have a moderating influence on the males.* But these measures were obviously inadequate and Mill looked at some methods of electing in two stages, though none of these were appropriate. He approved of the current method of electing American Senators,† given the right type of Federal Constitution. He therefore advocated a system of plural voting based on the level of individual educational attainment which would balance the votes of the less educated, but would not be carried to the level which would allow the more educated to practise class legislation themselves.[23]

PARTICIPATION

Mill's fears and his problem would be resolved if allegiance to the system could be assured. Participation is the means by which, he thought, government power may be restricted and it also has the educational effect of explaining the purposes and methods of government functions by exercising them. Mill points this out;

> It is also to be borne in mind that political machinery does not act of itself. As it is first made, so it has to be worked, by men, and even by ordinary men. It needs, not their simple acquiescence, but their active participation; and must be adjusted to the capacities and qualities of such men as are available.

This implied three conditions. The people for whom the system is intended must be willing to accept it. They must be willing to maintain it and they must be willing and able to help it to fulfil its purposes.[24] Why should people be willing to embrace such a system? Because:

> ... The rights and interests of any and every person are only secure from being disregarded when the person interested is himself able, and habitually disposed, to stand up for them.[25]

So self-interest and self-protection, the utilitarian aspects of participation, will force or encourage people to take part. Once they have joined other

---

*Mill's fear about class legislation have proved groundless, but there is some evidence to suggest that the influence of female electors may have helped to ensure this.

†Until 1913 Senators were elected (two for each state regardless of the size of the state) by their State Legislature and not by popular vote.

participants, they will identify with them and with the system because participation has an integrative effect. Furthermore,

> ... the only government which can fully satisfy all the exigencies of the social state is one in which the whole people participate; that any participation, even in the smallest public function, is useful. That participation should everywhere be as great as the general degree of improvement of the community will allow; and that nothing less can be ultimately desirable than the admission of all to a share in the sovereign power of the state.[26]

Everyone should join in because this is the only way in which full satisfaction can be achieved, menial tasks are useful but workers should not expect to participate fully until the whole community improves sufficiently to bring it to a higher stage of development. It is ultimately desirable though not necessarily ultimately possible that the whole electorate should be sovereign. Participation promised allegiance to the system because it brought educational improvement, it integrated people into the system because they identified themselves with it and it was self-sustaining because it satisfied people's need to belong. Mill hoped that this would be enough to curb any desire to control.

REPRESENTATION

> But since all cannot, in a community exceeding a single small town, participate personally in any but some very minor portions of the public business, it follows that the ideal type of government must be representative.[27]

Representation by an educated élite who would know what was in the best interests of the polity and would benevolently administer it.

References

1. Maurice Cranston (translator), J. J. Rousseau, *The Social Contract* (1968), Bk. II, Chap. 7, pp. 84 ff.
2. *Ibid.*, Bk. III, Chap. 1, p. 101.
3. *Ibid.*, Bk. I, Chap. 6, p. 61.
4. *Ibid.*, Bk. I, p. 62.
5. *Ibid.*, Bk. IV, Chap. 3, p. 156.
6. *Ibid.*, Bk. III, Chap. 4, pp. 112 and 114 *passim*.
7. *Ibid.*, Bk. III, Chap. 3, p. 111.
8. *Ibid.*, Bk. III, Chap. 5, p. 115.
9. *Ibid.*, Bk. III, Chap. 4, p. 113.

10. *Ibid.*, Bk. III, Chap. 4, p. 113.
11. *Ibid.*, Bk. III, Chaps. 10 and 11 *passim.*
12. *Ibid.*, Bk. IV, Chap. 8, p. 186.
13. Professor Talmon, *The Origins of Totalitarian Democracy.*
14. George D. H. Cole, *Guild Socialism Re-stated* (1920), p. 9.
15. *Ibid.*, pp. 32 and 33.
16. *Ibid.*, pp. 33 and 34.
17. *Ibid.*, pp. 71 ff.
18. *Ibid.*, p. 76.
19. John S. Mill, *Utilitarianism, Liberty and Representative Government,* "Representative Government", p. 254, Everyman, 1910.
20. *Ibid.*, "On Liberty", p. 165.
21. *Ibid.*, p. 164.
22. *Ibid.*, "Representative Government", p. 254.
23. *Ibid.*, p. 286.
24. *Ibid.*, p. 177.
25. *Ibid.*, p. 208.
26. *Ibid.*, p. 217.
27. *Ibid.*, pp. 217 and 218.

CHAPTER 3

The Labour Party as a Political Entity

The Gift of the 'Lawgivers'

The present constitution of the Labour Party which has undergone only modernising amendments in over half a century was drafted by Sidney Webb and Arthur Henderson in 1917 and approved following minor amendments by the Party Conference in February 1918. Sidney Webb's proposals for the Party's future policy objectives embodied in his policy document 'Labour and the New Social Order' submitted with it, was approved at the first Conference convened under the new constitution in June 1918.

It is not now possible to assess to what exact degree these two 'Lawgivers' were influenced in their task by political philosophers, Webb's father was ". . . an ardent supporter of John Stuart Mill's candidature at Westminster in 1865"[1] and, "Webb was a disciple of John Stuart Mill",[2] but even so, the structural similarities between the Party Constitution and Rousseau's requirements for a self-governing state when the physical characteristics of size and organisational structures are taken into consideration, are remarkable.

Webb and Henderson saw that if the Party was to gain the strength and influence it needed to adequately promote the interests of Labour which was its primary purpose, it would be necessary to ". . . transform the Labour Party from a Federation able to act only through its affiliated societies, into a nationally organised Party, with a local party of its own in every parliamentary constituency".[3] Participation, therefore, could not just be a means to ensure the democratisation of the new movement, or just a useful tool to promote membership integration, or merely an educative factor, although it would perform all of these functions. But it (participation) was absolutely essential for the growth of the new Party

16

itself, and for its electoral organisation which was vital to ensure the registration and gain the ballot-box allegiance of the vast new electorate, including the newly enfranchised women over 30 years of age who had now become fully fledged electors.

Participation by the new individual membership was a basically essential function in promoting the Party's purpose. And therefore, the internal role given to it by participatory democratic theorists, useful and desirable, even essential as it was, must have received only secondary consideration from the 'Lawgivers', who were more concerned with pragmatic considerations than by democratic theory. If participation was a vitally necessary requirement, it became necessary to provide the conditions which would attract and retain the participants without alienating the existing federal societies affiliated to the Party.

The Trade Unions were becoming more attuned to socialist thinking and the old Liberal element was dying off, many trade unionists were openly advocating Workers' Control of Industry and a move was already afoot to form a separate Trade Union Labour Party based on the Trade Union Congress. At the same time most trade unionists thought of the Independent Labour Party and the other Socialist societies as dangerously revolutionary, while in the popular mind, confusion existed concerning the separate roles of the Labour and Liberal parties.

The Labour Party therefore had to be given a separate ideological identity which would appeal not only to the men and women of the working class, but also to those members of the middle classes who wished to see a fairer, juster society. This was necessary if the Party was to be seen as a future government instead of an organisation merely wishing to influence the law as it affected organised labour and if it was to be accepted by both the Trade Unions and the ILP.

The result was a constitution (handed down by 'Lawgivers' especially commissioned for the task) which was avowedly Socialist, though of an evolutionary rather than a revolutionary nature.

The Labour Party Constitution

This lays down general laws for the government of the Party and its members, it lays down the purposes and principles for which and by which the Party exists and the method by which the constitution and the programme may be amended. The result conforms very closely to Rousseau's requirements for the 'General Will'. The General Will must compromise only *general* laws,[4] i.e. those laws designed especially for his 'Republic' by the specially chosen 'Lawgiver' to operate within the carefully studied physical and demographic conditions pertaining to the 'polity'. The 'Lawgiver' is influenced to a great extent by pragmatic considerations because the civil religion, the ideological basis of the state is determined by Rousseau's sovereign.[5] Here the Labour Party Constitution differs, Clause IV which embodies the Party's objects and outlines its ideology having been designed to promote evolutionary socialism in conformity with Webb's belief in the 'inevitability of gradualism'[6] was part of the 'Lawgivers' gift. The General Will, as a whole, had to be accepted unanimously, if anyone repudiated it, they denied the polity and must be treated as foreigners. But if they continued in residence after the state was instituted, this implied consent, "to inhabit the territory is to submit to the sovereign".[7] The General Will therefore is a body of permanent law, the acceptance of which confers sovereignty on the whole body politic and it may only be amended with the acquiescence of all. Other laws and policies, dealing with specific matters, which are designed to implement the constitution and/or advance its ideological purpose, which are necessarily of a less permanent, more changeable nature, being subject to supercession due: to their own implementation, to changes in circumstances, or, to changes in the majority opinion regarding their efficacy, etc. (e.g. the Programme of the Labour Party), are not themselves part of the 'General Will'. They are of a secondary or administrative nature,[8] although they may express the 'Majority Will' for the time being, while they are in force.[9] But many such issues become identified in the minds of some individual members, with the purpose of the Labour Party, or with what they think is, or should be, the 'General Will', especially if parliamentary action appears to be a retreat from something they associate with the Party's purpose, e.g. the original imposition of prescription charges within the Health Service. This sort of mental association is undoubtedly part of the reason for the massive decline in individual membership since it reached its peak figure of over 1 million in 1952 to about two-thirds of that figure in 1974.

The Constitution and the Membership

All individual members of the Labour Party and all its affiliated organisations *must* agree to accept the Constitution, Programme, Principles and Policy of the Party and new members joining must sign an application form to that effect. All membership cards carry paragraph 4, which is the best known and most revered tenet of the Party's ideological faith and is part of Clause IV of the Constitution.

At the 1959 Annual Conference, Hugh Gaitskell, at that time Party Leader, attempted to change and 'modernise' Clause IV. The Conference overwhelmingly repudiated the attempt and during the following year Gaitskell was subjected to many attacks on his Socialist integrity. Feeling in the Party was extremely high and Gaitskell had to retreat from the idea although the 1960 Conference accepted "a new declaration . . . explanatory of the old Clause, not a substitute for it".[10] The Constitution and Principles are analogous to the 'General Will' and the 'civil religion' respectively, while the programme and policy of the Party, being the means by which the Constitution and Principles are implemented, constitute administrative decisions.

The methods of amending the Constitution on the one hand and the Programme on the other are essentially different. Proposals to amend either can originate with the National Executive Committee or with the membership, but in the case of policy changes, the NEC may submit policy documents to delegates for the approval of Annual Conference without allowing time for these to be discussed by the membership at large. This is not and never has been the case with Constitutional Amendments or Supplements which have always been included with resolutions in the circulated Agenda.* The method and timing for the submission of constitutional amendments has varied, the most recent change being in 1968 when the time cycle was changed from three years to one, but the submission of a rule amendment required the sacrifice of the ability to submit a policy resolution.

*The reorganisation of Local Government implemented in 1973 meant that a reorganisation of the Party Structure was necessary. "58 area consultations with representatives of constituency Labour Parties were held between June and December 1973. Each consultation was conducted by the National Agent or an
(continued on page 20)

A rule amendment must now be submitted direct to the NEC which will make proposals concerning it in the following year and it must be circulated in the first agenda for the year in which the Conference will consider it.[11] Both types of motion require a two-thirds majority; for a rule amendment to secure its implementation, and for a policy motion to gain its automatic inclusion in the Party Programme. But inclusion in the programme does not necessarily ensure inclusion in an election manifesto, or implementation by a Labour Government.

The Party Programme

The procedure for dealing with the Party Programme is laid down in Clause V of the Party Constitution and this gives the power to decide which policy items from the Programme shall be included in the Manifesto and how issues raised by the Election but not included in the Manifesto shall be dealt with, to the National Executive Committee and the Parliamentary Committee of the Parliamentary Labour Party. This has been the cause of much dissatisfaction to sections of the membership over the years, because, in effect it gives a large measure of autonomy regarding the implementation of policy to the leadership of the Parliamentary Party (hereafter PLP), while in opposition, and this devolves on the Cabinet when a Labour Government is in office. Additionally, virtually anything can be held to have been raised by an election, during the period in which a government is in office by virtue of that election. It is true that the constitution involves the NEC in the process, but, it is argued, the PLP is

(continued from page 19)
Assistant National Agent. A total of some 2700 party activists from 570 constituency parties attended. In addition the National Agent attended a further 8 area consultations with trade union officers. Consultations were also held with the National Labour Women's Advisory Committee, the Co-op Party executive, full-time agents and the Regional Organising Staff. To assist these consultations, a consultative document was produced.

A detailed report of these consultations was presented to the National Executive Committee which decided on proposals for structure and other matters, following which revised rules were approved. A summary of the report, details of the committee's proposals and the draft revised rules are contained in a separate booklet which will be presented to the Annual Party Conference for consideration." (*The Labour Party Annual Report 1974*, p. 36).[12]

the body which deals with parliamentary legislation and therefore it can always have the last word.

This PLP autonomy is not due to careless drafting of the constitution, it was deliberately contrived by the 'Lawgivers' to give continued effect and added strength to an Annual Conference resolution passed in 1907, and it has been upheld on every occasion on which the principle has been challenged since its inception.

In 1960 the NEC issued a pamphlet, *Constitution of the Labour Party*, written by the then General Secretary, Mr. Morgan Phillips, 'to clarify the position'. In 1907 there were 17 resolutions ". . . which made demands for Parliamentary action in the form of 'instructions', to Labour M.P.s" on the Conference Agenda. The NEC

> appreciated that the Parliamentary Party would be quite unable to carry out all these 'instructions' . . . even from the point of view of time alone. In addition it was essential to retain a broad measure of freedom of action for tactical purposes. The Committee therefore proposed to Conference that:
> "resolutions instructing the Parliamentary Party as to their action in the House of Commons be taken as the opinions of Conference, on the understanding that the time and method of giving effect to those instructions be left to the Party in the House in conjunction with the National Executive."
> This declaration was carried and still remains the definitive statement of the relationship between the PLP and the Party as a whole . . . Annual Conference does not instruct the Parliamentary Party; it does instruct the National Executive Committee. To ensure co-ordination, the latter is specifically instructed by the Constitution to consult with the Parliamentary Party at the beginning of each Session and on any other occasion which warrants it. These arrangements have normally led to the maintenance of a common agreed policy.[13]

This at that time (1960) was true, but during the later years of the 1964/70 Labour Government, the NEC's opinions seemed to carry very little weight with the Cabinet. But the body of the PLP in response to grave disquiet within the Labour Movement, demonstrated in 1969, that it retains the power to curb its own leadership. This became apparent when the Chief Whip, Bob Mellish, assessed that many of its members would refuse to vote for 'penal sanctions' based on the White Paper *In Place of Strife*. In 1969 also a special Policy Co-ordinating sub-committee composed of members of the NEC and the Labour Cabinet, which was set up in an attempt to clear misunderstanding between the membership and the Labour Government, sat for the first time.[14] Subsequently, the NEC report to the Annual Conference of 1975 states:

> WORK OF SUB-COMMITTEES   The Home Policy Committee has a number of standing sub-committees whose function is to assist the National Executive Committee in the development of policy, and to be available for advice on specific issues. These sub-committees, which include all the relevant Ministers among their memberships, also enable the National Executive Committee to keep under review the progress of implementing the Manifesto, whilst at the same time providing a 'sounding Board' for any policies coming forward from the Government Departments. So successful has been this arrangement of standing sub-committees, that the original six sub-committees, established in 1971, have been expanded to eleven, and now cover almost the whole field of domestic policy. The sub-committees are now working towards the preparation of the 1976 version of Labour's Programme.[15]

On April 1st, 1974 the Liaison Committee of the PLP was restructured to take in back bench members for the first time.

> THE FUNCTIONS   1. The main function of the committee is to maintain an effective two-way channel of communication between the Government and the back-benchers in both Houses.[16]

The 1975 Parliamentary Report to the Annual Conference states:

> LIAISON COMMITTEE   When the Labour Party is in Government the Parliamentary Party appoints a Liaison Committee representative of both the Government Front Bench and Labour Back Benchers. The Chairman is elected by the whole Parliamentary Party and is a back bencher. The back bench representatives, are elected only by the back benchers. The Government representatives, who always include the Leader of the House and the Chief Whip, are appointed by the Prime Minister. The back bench Labour Peers elect their own representative.[17]

Justification of Occupational Autonomies

The Labour Party has only one real product and this is its Policies, these are produced for use outside its own parameters, i.e. to produce legislation in the British Parliament and Local Authorities, and, although the application of its policies will affect its own membership, the policies are intended to benefit the populace at large. The Labour Party therefore manufactures the bulk of its production for export.

In order to market its products, like any exporting Nation State, it maintains the equivalent of:

A large Foreign Office Staff or Trade Delegations – these comprise: the individual Members of Parliament and Labour Councillors.*

Ambassadors – analogous to – Ministers or Members of the Shadow Cabinet.

A Foreign or Trade Minister – who also happens to be – The Party Leader.

Rousseau's 'Lawgiver' legislating for a Republic which depended wholly on exports or Foreign Treaties/Trade Agreements, would surely enable its exporting authority or Foreign Office to carry out its task "within the Constitution/General Will" without specific government instruction on the nature and timing of every transaction in the foreign market or every aspect of negotiation, providing that their overall activities were periodically ratified.

> This does not mean that the whole body cannot incur obligations to other nations, so long as those obligations do not infringe the contract.[18]

The Parliamentary Labour Party and the National Executive Committee both make an Annual Report on their activities to the Annual Conference of the Party, and these are available for ratification or censure.

The Annual Conference

The Annual Conference is the Government of the Labour Party. Mr. R. T. McKenzie disputes this. In his book, *British Political Parties*, he takes up Clement Atlee's statement ". . . the Labour Party Conference is in fact a Parliament of the movement." (Atlee, C. R., *The Labour Party* in *Perspective*, London, 1937, p. 93) and avers that the Annual Conference cannot be a Parliament because it does not control the whole movement (this is a reference to the autonomy of the PLP). The Conference, of course, is *not* a Parliament but not just for this reason, it is not a Parliament because *it is not sovereign.* Sovereignty lies in the membership. The Conference is convened and elects its own administration (the NEC) in accordance with Clauses VI . . . VII . . . and VIII of the Constitution. It

*Labour Groups of Councillors enjoy an autonomy similar to that of the PLP in respect of Constituency Labour Parties.

meets annually in a different place each year although these places have become fewer over the years because of the increasing size of the assembly.

Rousseau advocated that in large states the General Assembly should meet in different places and this the Annual Conference does. But it is *not* the Sovereign assembly of the Party. The Sovereign meets in thousands of different places every month in the Constituency Labour Party branches and affiliated organisations, here it legislates and produces local and national policy. Once in every year, branches and affiliated organisations are invited to submit a motion for Annual Conference to their Constituency Labour Party (hereafter CLP), which considers their motions and forwards one, or a composite of several to the General Secretary of the Labour Party, as a motion for inclusion on the Agenda for Annual Conference. These motions since 1968 may be either a Policy Resolution or a motion to amend the Constitution.* Delegates to CLPs are elected or selected yearly, often on a rotation basis to allow members the maximum opportunity to participate in constituency party government. Delegates to Annual Conference are frequently elected on the same principle, members who have attended Annual Conference within a certain number of years not being available for nomination. In Constituency Parties where a secretary is employed the motions which are received from Branches, etc., are usually circulated in good time for delegates to be briefed on their organisation's view concerning them. In many cases, due mainly to shortage of money, this does not happen and in a very few impoverished constituencies, a delegate to Conference cannot even be sent.

The NEC compiles a first Agenda which contains all the Policy Motions submitted by CLPs and Affiliated Organisations and all motions to amend the Constitution which will be taken that year. Amendments may now be submitted on the Policy Motions but not on the Rule Amendments. A final Agenda is then circulated and many Parties supply these to their Branches because it is on this Agenda that the Delegate to Annual Conference is mandated.

In the author's experience, Labour Party members treat constitutional amendments as important and the delegate has invariably been mandated on these. If the constituency submits a Policy Resolution, the Delegate has an automatic mandate to speak on it if called, or support any composite

*See above, pp. 19, 20.

containing it. Delegates are usually mandated *for* or *against* groupings of Motions which are likely to be composited, and which the General Management Committee of the CLP thinks are important. Important single Motions are treated in the same way. The Delegate is quite often left unmandated on resolutions which do not concern his party deeply, or when the General Management Committee thinks that the delegate has a sufficient knowledge of its views.

Trade unionists who pay the political levy may also submit motions through their union branch, usually to the Annual Conference of the Union Party to be considered for the Union's resolution to Annual Conference. It is usually at their Conference that the Union's delegation is elected. Only union members who are also individual members of the Party may serve on the delegation or attend official meetings of the Party at any level.

Annual Conference which comprises delegates elected annually and mandated on how they shall vote; to elect the NEC, on policy matters, and on amendments to the Constitution, therefore governs the whole of the Party under the General Will of the Sovereign membership.

Rousseau thought that if separate institutional interests existed within a state, they should be many and of roughly equal size. The block vote of each Trade Union may therefore have caused him some dismay at first sight, but, they do not seem to have been used to maintain overwhelming Trade Union control of the Executive, and no matter how large the union, it is only entitled to one resolution to Annual Conference.

The Labour Party Constitution provides very considerable opportunities for the participation of its members in both the government and the decision-making processes of the Party. It is too large and complex an organisation for its government to be a 'direct democracy' in Rousseau's terms, but it is a very democratic form of his best of all government, i.e. elective aristocracy. A government which meets in different parts of the country for 5 days each year, which is subject to annual change, which annually elects its administration (NEC) by members who are subject to mandation by the sovereign, must qualify for his more practical use of the

... there is no government so liable to civil war and internecine strife as is democracy or popular government, for there is none which has so powerful and constant a tendency to change to another form or which demands so much vigilance and courage to maintain it unchanged.[20]

term 'democracy'. Rousseau warned,

The Labour Party has often been classified by the press and communications media as being in a constant state of civil war and internecine strife and it has managed to retain this image since it received its Constitution from the 'Lawgivers'.

Many people would hold that the last few years of the 1964/70 Labour government showed an increasing tendency towards Oligarchy in the Cabinet's attitude to the extra-parliamentary party. But the PLP's eventual response to this along with the formation and subsequent development of the Policy sub-committee and the back bench capability introduced into the PLP Liaison Committee show that the Party has the mechanism and the will and intention to resist it.

Ochlocracy* is undoubtedly arrested by the general acceptance of the Autonomy of the PLP and the fact that unlike the citizens of a Nation State, a Labour Party member can find asylum in the outside world without uprooting himself and his family from their home, if he thinks that the General Will has ceased to coincide with his own 'true will'.

References

1. Drake, Barbara and Cole, M. (eds.), *Our Partnership*, Beatrice Webb (1948), p. 3.
2. Pelling, Henry, *Origins of the Labour Party*, Oxford (1966), p. 37.
3. Cole, G. D. H., *A History of the Labour Party from 1914*, Routledge & Keegan Paul Ltd. (1948), p. 45.
4. *Op. cit.*, Rousseau, Bk. II, Chaps. 4 and 6 *passim*.
5. *Ibid.*, Bk. IV, Chap. 8, p. 186.
6. *Op. cit.*, Pelling, p. 76.
7. *Op. cit.*, Rousseau, Bk. IV, Chap. 2, p. 153.
8. *Ibid.*, Bk. II, Chap. 2, p. 70, and Chaps. 4 and 6 *passim*.
9. *Ibid.*, Bk. II, Chap. 3, p. 72.
10. Wilson, Harold, *The Relevance of British Socialism*, Weidenfeld and Nicolson (1964), p. 6.
11. *The Labour Party Annual Report 1968*, pp. 9 and 10.
12. *The Labour Party Annual Report 1974*, p. 36.
13. Phillips, Morgan, *Constitution of the Labour Party*, The Labour Party (1960).
14. *The Labour Party Annual Report 1969*, p. 29.
15. *The Labour Party Annual Report 1975*, p. 34.
16. *The Labour Party Annual Report 1974*, p. 90.
17. *The Labour Party Annual Report 1975*, p. 56.
18. *Op. cit.*, Rousseau, Bk. I, Chap. 7, p. 63.
19. McKenzie, Robert T., *British Political Parties*, Heinemann (1964), p. 485.
20. *Op. cit.*, Rousseau, Bk. III, Chap. 4, p. 113.

*Mob rule.

CHAPTER 4

Constituency Labour Party Branches

The Constituency Labour Party Branch is the Party's membership base.* The member resides or is registered as a parliamentary or local government elector in the area covered by his/her† branch. No person may be a member of more than one Branch of one CLP. The Branch area may cover an electoral ward, a part of a ward or a number of wards. In County Constituencies it may cover a small town or a village or a number of villages. CLP branches compromise the entire individual membership of the Labour Party. No one who is not a member of a CLP Branch may take part in the internal‡ meetings or functions of the Party (except for Women's Councils, see below, p. 33). Supporters who are not members are, of course, both allowed and encouraged to help with election work, although they are usually exhorted to become individual members.

The Branches themselves are composed entirely of individual members and do not accept delegates from any source. The Trade Unionist may serve in the CLP Branch, as may the co-operator, or the Fabian or any member of an affiliated Socialist society, but only in the capacity of an individual member, not as a delegate.

Like G. D. H. Cole's guildsman, the member may represent his fellow members or appoint them to represent him in respect of numerous varying interests at different levels within the Labour Movement. He may participate fully in every aspect of the work of his CLP Branch and may appoint delegates or be appointed as a delegate to represent the Branch on the General Management Committee of his Constituency Labour Party. Concurrently he is represented at this same level by delegates from any or

---

*See Appendix A.
†Henceforth, allusion to the male should be taken to include the female.
‡As opposed to public meetings or joint meetings with other bodies.

all of the organisations of which he is a member and which are affiliated to his CLP. As a Trade Unionist; from his own T. U. Branch if it affiliates to the CLP, as a co-operater or member of a Socialist organisation; from any local affiliated branch of the relevant society. Each of these representatives must belong to a Party Branch affiliated to his CLP. And so, views and ideas expressed in a Branch of an affiliated organisation may become widely discussed through an informal transmission of ideas throughout the local movement and beyond.

Female members through their Women's sections and Young Socialist members through their Y/S Branches may be additionally represented on their CLP.

CLP Branches under the supervision of the Executive Committee of the Constituency Party also select candidates for election to the appropriate Local Authority. The candidates must be individual members of the Labour Party but may live anywhere within the Local Government Electoral Area. CLP Branches, District and County Labour Parties, elect their officers, executive committees and delegates annually.

The CLPs resemble Cole's Town or Township Communes. They are completely self-managing and their Executive Committees comprise members elected from delegates nominated by and representing each particular affiliated interest in proportions laid down in their rules. Their officers are elected from delegates nominated by any or all of the Affiliated organisations as also sometimes are only delegates additionally elected to carry out some specialist function. The CLPs elect delegates to represent them: Locally, at meetings of the Labour Group of Councillors;* at the Local Trades Council; on intramovement liaison committees; on District Labour Parties where District Council boundaries are different to the CLP's Parliamentary boundaries;† on County Labour Parties; on Borough Local Government Committees in the Greater London Area‡ and on any citizens' group on which the CLP may be represented; Regionally, delegates are appointed to the appropriate Regional Council of the Labour Party from CLPs and County Labour parties; and, Nationally, a CLP delegate is elected to represent the individual membership at Annual Conference.

*Directly where District Council and Parliamentary Constituency boundaries are coterminous and through District and County Labour Parties otherwise.
†See Appendix B.
‡See Appendix C.

The Trade Unions, Co-operative and Socialist Societies which affiliate to the Party at Constituency level send representatives to their own district, area or regional organisation and these affiliate and send delegates to the Regional Council of the Party.

The process is repeated at National level and delegates are sent to the Annual Conference where the National Executive Committee is elected in fixed numbers, representing the individual membership and the affiliated interests.

Cole's ideas were designed to promote social justice and to give people as much control as possible over their total environment. He, like Rousseau, thought that a high degree of institutional equality was necessary, that in these conditions socialism could flourish and sustain itself because participation would educate people about their own problems and the problems of others. In working together for the benefit of all, they would come to identify themselves with the system and become intellectually as well as physically integrated into it, thereby creating a polity which would sustain itself through the increasing political awareness which would encourage the total involvement of the people.

There is a close analogy between Cole's model of a participatory socialist polity and the participatory/representative abilities of the individual members of the Labour Party because they share a similar federal structure and are based on the same social institutions. Cole believed that no single person could represent his guildsman completely as a man. Here the member's different interests and ideas may be represented by different people who severally share his interests while he may represent others in furthering the interests they share with him. This greatly extends his influence in the conduct of matters affecting him or of interest to him.

R. T. McKenzie points out that less than 10% of the Labour Party membership attend their (*sic*) Ward meetings. But he makes no assessment of the proportion of members involved in election work during a campaign, or of people who 'work for the party', e.g. as fund raisers, etc.[1]

The introduction to the Labour Party booklet *Party Organisation*, 1966 edition,[2] states:

> ... the rules governing constituency and (sic) Local Labour Parties state clearly that the objects of the Party are "to unite the forces of Labour within

the Constituency and to secure the return of Labour representatives to Parliament and Local Government bodies."

Party organisation is the key to power and it is only by maintaining efficient organisation, from which electoral machinery is built, that the Party's objects can be attained. The main task to ensure success in a Constituency is to harness the enthusiasm of members to work which has to be done to create a dynamic party.

And the foreword to the booklet by Sara E. Barker, the then National Agent, finishes with the sentence: "It should be remembered always that the victory of ideals must be organised.'

These extracts seem to indicate that the official view of the role of the ordinary Party member is that his participation is required to promote the Party to office and if possible to keep it there.

The role accords well with J. S. Mill's ideas on the correct functions of the mass of a political movement, faith in the leadership and involvement with the lowly tasks which will broaden their grasp on mainly local policy matters, integrate them into the movement by establishing and maintaining a group identity, and sustaining their efforts by a belief in its essential character in the general advancement of the movement.

References

1.   *Op. cit.*, McKenzie, p. 547.
2.   *Party Organisation* (1966 edition), published by the Labour Party.

CHAPTER 5

Women's Sections

> Although . . . the Labour Party seeks to minimise sex differences, it has found it necessary, to set up organisations within the Party expressly limited to women.[1]

In 1918 the Women's Labour League, which had been formed in London on the initiative of the National Union of Railwaywomen's Guilds in 1906 and was affiliated to the Labour Party in 1908, was officially disbanded because its members were now able to become individual members of the Labour Party under the new constitution and to join the Women's sections which the amended rules made provision for.[2]

> In addition to being attached to their local or Ward Parties,* individual women members shall be organised in women's sections, acting in accordance with regulations sanctioned by the National Executive Committee. Women's sections may be organised on constituency, local party or ward basis. In order to meet special local circumstances, a women's section may cover more than one ward within a constituency, or may cover only part of a ward, local party or polling district area.[3]

The individual woman member has an additional avenue of representation to her male counterpart which prima facie is discriminatory in her favour. Women's sections are entitled to representation on the General committees and usually the Executive committees of the CLPs to which their members are affiliated and on District and County Labour Parties.

Since 1951 women members have been represented on Regional Executive committees through Women's Advisory councils and since 1969 through Women's councils. Since 1969 also, CLPs have been entitled to appoint an extra (woman) delegate to Annual Conference if more than 1500 of their members are women (previously 2500), and there are five

*Now CLP Branches.

seats held by individual women members on the NEC. But these are subject to nomination and election by the whole of Conference. Additionally, women have an advisory role to the NEC through the National Women's Advisory Council and the Women's Annual Conference. The published figures for individual membership are unreliable for a number of reasons, but they are all we have and an analysis of them shows that from 1956 onwards, women's membership has hovered around 42% of the total. Their representation at various levels within the main body of the Party nowhere seems to reach anything like this proportion.

> Although no analysis exists it appears that in the majority of constituencies and on the General Management Committee and Executive Committee there are more men than women. It is perhaps only at grass roots level where the actual chores are being done for the Party, that the total number of women may equal or exceed that of men.[4]

The Simpson 'Report on Party Organisation' recommendation, that an extra woman delegate to Annual Conference be allowed to CLPs having a female membership of 1500 or over, was implemented, but this seems to have made no impact.

An analysis of Appendix XIV, pp. 235–251, of the *1956 Annual Report* shows:

Total no. of delegates from Federations and CLPs	= 518
Total no. of Women delegates from Federations and CLPs	= 107
∴ Percentage of delegates who were women	= 20.5%

Whereas for 1970 and 1971 after the increased representation:

1970 total no. of delegates from Federations and CLPs	= 497
Total no. of Women delegates from Federations and CLPs	= 90
∴Percentage of delegates who were women	= 18.1%

1971 total no. of delegates from Federations and CLPs	= 530
Total no. of Women delegates from Federations and CLPs	= 99
∴ Percentage of delegates who were women	= 18.7%[5]

An analysis of the List of Delegates to Annual Conference at Blackpool 1975 confirms that the increased capability to appoint women delegates has not been effective.

1975 total no. of delegates from CLPs	= 524
Total no. of Women delegates from CLPs	= 85
∴ Percentage of delegates who were women	= 16.2%

than half of the delegates places which proportionally should be theirs at Annual Conference and considerably less than their proportionate share at other levels are occupied by women. During the entire history of the Parliamentary Labour Party, only four women have reached Cabinet Ministerial rank. Furthermore, the total number of women standing as Labour Party candidates at the General Elections in:

> 1970 was 29 out of a total of 630 or 4.6%, the number elected being
> 10 out of a total of 287 or 3.48%
> 1974 was 40 out of a total of 635 or 6.29%, the number elected being
> (Feb.)   13 out of a total of 301 or 4.3%
> 1974 was 50 out of a total of 635 or 7.87%, the number elected being
> (Oct.)   18 out of a total of 319 or 5.6%

The Labour Party has always had more female Parliamentary Candidates in General Elections than the Tories and their record of election successes is usually better. The Liberals have had more in the field but their record is abysmal.* The National Labour Women's advisory Council says: "Many women are convinced that their biological function is deliberately being exploited in order to keep them in a traditional, supportive role to their husbands."[11] This is undoubtedly true in many cases, but it is equally true in the author's experience, that many women elect to play a supportive role. It is also true that many Labour Party women who confine their activities to those organised by their Women's sections or by the Womens' organisation, feel as fulfilled in respect of their political activities as any female member of the Parliamentary labour Party.

The Women's Movement performs in a mainly educational and advisory role which makes a massive contribution to the increase of political awareness within the 'Polity' and this is a desirable function within each of the philosophers' models. Furthermore, Women's sections exhibit a high degree of participation in essential organisational tasks, without acting as a sectional competitive interest seeking governmental control. This is both educational and integrative, women who prefer to work mainly within the women's movement are highly integrated into it.

For Cole it also provides an additional avenue for self-expression and personal representation.

*See Appendix D.

the National Conference of Labour Women (the size of which would therefore be considerably increased) and other women's organisations.[6]

The Simpson Committee approved these recommendations and they were given effect by the 1968 Annual Conference and by December 1971, 198 Women's Councils* had been established. But the proposal to abolish the five women's seats on the NEC was turned down by the 1971 Annual Conference on the advice of the NEC which had been in receipt of very strong representations from the National Labour Women's Advisory Committee.[7] The National Conference of Labour Women has no policy-making powers.

> When the women's conference is over, the National Labour Women's Advisory Committee considers the resolutions which were remitted to the Committee and those not reached at the conference because of the time factor, as well as those which were carried. The Committee decides on the course of action to take arising from these resolutions and each organisation responsible for the resolutions is advised of the action taken.[8]
>
> ... resolutions from the Women's Conference have the same status as resolutions from constituency or local parties. The documents prepared by the research department as a result of prior discussion in the women's organisations have had little attention by the Party — despite their excellent nature and the fact that they have covered subjects not covered in depth by the Party, and have been widely accepted by outside bodies as being valuable social studies.[9]

The Women's Organisation has a supportive role in the Party and a great many women members feel that their particular role is to act as fund-raisers, to promote education, to act as recruiting agents, to promote social activities and to participate in election work. In fact, the majority of the Labour Party members of both sexes are within the range of those who pay their subscription and consider their duty done, to those who work very hard at election times, take part in social functions and help in fund raising, but never attend meetings. The members who attend branch meetings and/or women's sections are a minority, albeit a substantial minority of the total individual membership. At grass roots level " ... the total number of women may equal or exceed that of men".[10] But less than half of the delegates places which proportionally should be theirs at

*In the *1974 Annual Report* of the Labour Party, the NEC Report gives 220 as the figure for Women's Councils. And the *1975 Annual Report* p. 11, "... regrets that not all constituency parties are using the constitutional facilities to establish a Women's Council".

The Simpson Committee, which was obviously concerned about the low representation of women, also recommended the abolition of the five women's seats on the NEC. This appears contradictory but for many years there had been a growing pressure exerted not least by some of the more active women in the Party, for abolition of the women's organisations, on the grounds that women should participate fully in the Party, that they can only gain real equality if they repudiate both favourable and unfavourable discrimination.

The Report of the working party on Women's Organisation (May 1968) to the NEC " . . . recognises that a body of opinion within the Party takes the view that there is no longer such a need", but the scope and extent of voluntary women's organisations in the country led the working party to conclude that women of all educational and social levels apparently find value in meeting together, and that "many . . . women still feel the need for the additional political education and training that a women's organisation can provide", the working party was " . . . agreed that even greater political activity among women is required and there is a need for women's organisation within the Labour Party". It pointed to the tremendous amount of work done by the Women's Organisation in the field of political education, fund raising, election work and social activity.

At the moment there were 1425 Women's Sections, 173 Women's Constituency committees and Federations, 64 Women's Area Advisory Councils, a National Labour Women's Advisory Committee with 22 members, plus women members of the NEC, and the Labour Women's National Conference had an annual delegation between 400 and 500.

It recommended that the work of the Women's Organisation be extended by the initiation of Women's Councils which would take over the responsibilities of Women's Constituency Federations and Committees, and many of the functions of Women's Advisory Councils. The Councils would be composed of representatives from Women's Sections, informal groups, e.g. lunch and supper clubs, coffee circles, young mums groups, etc., whose members other than the officers and Women's Council representatives need not necessarily be individual party members, women in party organisations, women trade unionists, female members of affiliated organisations and women on Labour Groups of Councillors. The Women's Councils would appoint representatives to the Regional Women's Advisory Committees, the National Labour Women's Advisory Committee,

Mill would have approved because of the danger of under-representation of a minority, i.e. women, the provision of five seats, which at this time brings the women's representation on the NEC up to 7 or 25%. This might seem roughly proportional to the overall number of women in the Party if the total membership, i.e. affiliated trade unionists as well as individual members are taken into consideration. The attempt to increase the representation of women at Annual Conference by allowing them extra delegates for high membership seems to have failed.

But the ability of the Women's sections to govern their own affairs at local level, the raising usually of their own funds and their degree of voluntary participation in local affairs of the Party demonstrates that they accept the system, are willing to maintain it and that they help it to fulfil its purpose. Their additional freedom to choose whether to work in their CLP Branch and the main party as an active individual member or to confine themselves to the Women's movement together with the educational, supportive and advisory nature of that body would seem to fit in snugly with many of Mill's ideas concerning the role of a people under a representative form of government.

References

1. Sanderson-Furniss, Averil D., "The Citizenship of Women", *The Book of the Labour Party* (ed.) Herbert Tracey, Caxton Publishing Co. Ltd. (1925) Vol. II, p. 248.
2. Women's Organisation within the Labour Party, "History & Background", Unpublished Labour Party Document NAD/W/1/1/68.
3. *A Guide for Women's Sections*, The Labour Party (March 1965), p. 3.
4. Women & The Labour Party. "Statement by the National Labour Women's Advisory Council to the NEC." Unpublished L. P. Paper NAD/64/9/71 (R), p. 4.
5. *Ibid.*, p. 3.
6. Report of the Working Party on Women's Organisation (May 1968). Unpublished L. P. Document NAD/W/77/5/68.
7. *Op. cit.*, NAD/64/9/71 (R), p. 7.
8. *Op. cit.*, "A Guide for Women's Sections" p. 11.
9. *Op. cit.*, NAD/64/9/71 (R), p. 6.
10. *Ibid.*, p. 4.
11. *Ibid.*, p. 2.

CHAPTER 6

The Youth Movement

The Labour Party Youth Movement has had a very chequered career. It was officially initiated in a circular letter "ORGANISATION OF YOUTH"* dated August 1924, because the replies to an NEC questionnaire sent to all Labour Parties, ". . . in a very large majority of cases . . . were emphatically in favour of this work."

The work of the Young People's Sections was to be mainly recreational and educational although every encouragement would be given to participation in election work in order to take full advantage of the ". . . young people's energy and desire to serve". The purpose of the exercise was ". . . in order that they should more readily and enthusiastically take their place in the Labour Movement as they reach adult years". Age limits were 14–21 and the sections were to be attached to and form part of Local Labour Parties.†

In 1926 the movement was renamed 'The Labour League of Youth' and the upper age limit became 25 for those who were already individual party members or those who became individual members at 21. These innovations were introduced to counteract the ILP's recruitment campaign for its 'Guild of Youth'. A National Advisory Committee (NAC) was established in 1929 when the first Annual Conference of the Youth Movement was held.

The number of branches in the movement fluctuated yearly but the trend was upwards and there were 429 branches in 1934 when the Party Constitution was amended to allow two delegates (one of whom must be the National Chairman appointed by the League of Youth Conference) to attend the Annual Conference of the Party and to give the National

---

*See Appendix E.
†Local Labour Parties were the Party Organisations in small towns in County Constituencies phased out and replaced by CLP Branches in 1974.

Chairman a seat on the National Executive Committee. This in effect meant that he was elected *ex-officio*, a privilege enjoyed only by the Party Leader since 1929 and not accorded to the Deputy Leader until 1953.[1]

The seat was occupied in 1935 and suspended in 1936 when the NAC was disbanded and the League of Youth Conference was not convened because of Communist infiltration. The publication of *New Nation*, the League of Youth newspaper, was also suspended and it was decided that the upper age limit must revert to 21.

The 1937 Annual Conference of the Labour Party abolished the youth seat on the NEC and allocated responsibility for the Youth Movement to CLPs. Transport House published a Youth Newspaper called *Advance*.

Early in 1939 a new National Advisory Committee was appointed – six members by the NEC and eight elected at the League of Youth Conference. But later the Annual Conference of the Party accepted an NEC proposal that the NAC, which had been refused NEC permission to collaborate with other Youth Movements, and which was overtly supporting Stafford Cripps, who was later expelled from the Party because of his Popular Front activities, should, with the London and other Advisory Committees, be disbanded, and the League of Youth Conference be not convened.

Very few branches survived both this and the war and in 1946 Mr. Reg Underhill, then Administrative Assistant to the National Agent, took on the work of Youth Development. In 1949 Mr. Len Williams, the Assistant National Agent, became also the National Youth Officer, and a National Youth Consultative Committee was set up with two members from each region. In 1950 Regional Youth Advisory Committees were set up to service 788 Branches and 44 Area Federations, and the League of Youth reached the peak of its organisational strength in 1951 with 806 Branches, but thereafter it declined rapidly.

The number of branches had dropped to 670 in 1952 and by 1955 only 237 branches and 13 Federations remained. Response to the requests for the appointment of delegates was so poor that arrangements for the League of Youth Conference had to be cancelled. The National and Regional machinery was dismantled because it was felt that there was a superstructure without sufficient foundation. In 1956 the branches reverted to Youth Sections attached to Local Parties and Mr. Alan Williams was appointed National Youth Officer. The decline continued. By

1959 only 262 sections remained and in April the NEC appointed a Working Party to look into Youth Organisation. The Working Party reported in December with proposals for a Youth Movement to be called the Young Socialists.

January 1960 saw the launching of the Y/S with full Regional and Federation machinery and 578 branches blossomed. But, almost immediately, the Socialist Labour League started its Trotskyite infiltration of the movement. In November that year Reg Underhill was appointed Assistant National Agent and Chief Youth Officer. The year 1961 saw the first Y/S Conference attended by 381 delegates and a National Committee was elected to represent 707 branches, 55 Federations and 9 Regional Committees. In 1962 there were 722 branches and 448 Youth Officers appointed by CLPs plus 60 Federations and a Y/S member served on the Executive Committee of every Regional Council of the Labour Party.

But, in 1962 also, the Trotskyite publication *Keep Left* was proscribed and four members of the Y/S National Committee had their membership suspended pending inquiries into their activities.

Three of the suspended members were expelled from the Party in 1963. There were now 769 branches, 459 Youth Officers, 57 Federations and 12 Regional Committees. By 1964 the number of branches had dropped back to 722 and a Y/S attempt to mount an unofficial lobby of Parliament on Unemployment was taken over by the NEC and converted to a march, followed by a lobby and a marathon meeting.

Thereafter the Trotskyite activity became much intensified, six members of the National Committee mounted a campaign inpugning both Party Leadership and Policy on the eve of the General Election.

Meetings of the National Committee were suspended, many branches were closed and some Y/S members were expelled by local parties.

In 1965 the Socialist Labour League set up its own Youth Organisation taking over the name Young Socialists and its National Committee included some of the people expelled by local parties. The Y/S rules were amended, the name being changed to the Labour Party Young Socialists, the Federations were disbanded and the National Committee had to be appointed by Regional Council Executive Committees after consultation with the Y/S Regional Committees. A Conference was held in 1965 on the basis of the revised rules.

The number of branches continued to fluctuate annually but hereafter the trend was downwards. 1965 – 605, 1966 – 571, 1967 – 576, 1968 – 533 and 1969 – 386.

The Chairman of the National Committee was appointed to the Youth Subcommittee of the NEC in 1967 and the Y/S publication *Left* was published from October 1968 onwards without any censorship.

The Simpson Committee of Enquiry into Party Organisation recommended that CLPs be allowed to appoint an extra delegate to Annual Conference, who must be a Young Socialist, for every 100 Y/S members (previously 200) of the CLP, and also made recommendations which would allow Y/S members to appoint their own delegate, submit their own resolutions and amendments, from their own branch on their own responsibility, to their own National Conference without interference by their CLP.

Additionally they recommended: that Regional Conference of Branches be allowed to discuss matters of Regional concern peculiar to young people and to appoint its own member of the National Committee. That two Y/S members be appointed to serve on each Regional Executive Committee of the Party; that CLPs having a branch or branches of the Y/S be allowed to appoint a member of the Y/S as an additional Delegate to the Annual Conference of the Regional Council; that the Y/S National Conference resolutions may now be on 'Subjects of General Interest', i.e. Policy; that their Conference Standing Orders Committee shall comprise two people elected at the last Conference and two members of the National Committee who shall elect their own chairman; and, that the Chairman of the National Conference shall be Chairman of the National Committee.

The Report says: "The net effect of all these changes would be to give to the Young Socialists more control of their own organisation than the Labour Youth Movement has ever enjoyed before."[2]

The appointment of a full-time National Youth Officer was also recommended, and the 1969 Annual Conference of the Labour Party accepted all the Committee's recommendations concerning Youth *in toto.*

In addition the NEC decided to recommend to the 1972 Annual Conference that a Y/S member again be elected to serve on the NEC.

It is noteworthy that while these recommendations give the Y/S much greater control over its own organisation, they do not significantly increase its ability to affect policy decisions at the Annual Conference of the Party.

The Y/S are allowed one resolution like any affiliated organisation and the women's movement. The age limits are now 15—25 and all Young Socialists must also be individual members of the Party.

The Advisory, educational, participatory and recreational purpose of the movement complements each of the philosophical models. Mill was concerned that the natural balance achieved by the spontaneous admixture of the old and the young, those whose position and reputation are made and those who have them still to make, should not be disturbed by artificial means,[3] and the promotion of the Y/S purpose could assist in overcoming the artificial barriers erected by the juxtaposition of maturity and immaturity in committee life.

It is difficult to see why the NEC so long resisted the Youth Movements' call for self-government in their own federal structure, because their power to influence policy lies in their power to influence their CLP branches, trade unions, socialist societies, women's sections, etc., through the multi-representational process. As a sectional interest they are not as powerful as any of the trade unions. Their numbers at Annual Conference could, of course, be disproportionate to others in the movement because of the special dispensation to CLPs on their behalf, but this is an educational and integrative concession only, in that it gives them no votes in respect of the Y/S, nor does it influence the card vote of their constituency party.

Fear of bad publicity and infiltration by foreign bodies (Communist, Trotskyite, etc.) have been the main reasons for NEC reluctance in this field. But the excessive claims of youthful enthusiasm at a Conference of Youth are unlikely to be given the same weight in the public mind as statements on behalf of the Party Conference, or as the NEC has feared.

Infiltration is, of course, more serious, but the Youth Movement has never been given the opportunity itself to attempt to contain this, and it seems to me that the ritual provision of martyrs has exactly the opposite effect to what the NEC has hoped to achieve.

CLPs in any case have the machinery to deal with the problem if it becomes too serious at local level. During the mid-1960s Trotskyite troubles, many CLPs, e.g. Oxford, quite firmly and efficiently excluded from membership those people who would not reaffirm their acceptance of the Constitution. But this action might never have been needed if the NEC had not reacted so violently. The advisory nature of the movement, given the power to administer itself under the constitution, could discourage disruptive militants who rely on excessive party governmental action as their main recruiting agent.*

References

1. *Op. cit.*, McKenzie, p. 517.
2. *The Labour Party Annual Report 1968*, pp. 372, 373, 379 and 380.
3. *Op. cit.*, Mill, *Representative Government*, p. 192.

*The circumstances of the appointment of Mr. Andrew (Andy) Bevan as Youth Officer have been summarised in Appendix F.

CHAPTER 7

Some Complaints which Seek to Deny or Modify the Labour Party's Claim to be a Participatory Democracy

Dr. R. T. McKenzie in his book *British Political Parties* considers the Labour Party's claim to intra-party democracy to be 'wilful self-deception'[1] and a dangerous fiction which renders it vulnerable to frequent paroxysms of internecine strife. He bases his thesis primarily on the belief that a PLP-dominated National Executive Committee was able to rely on the trade union 'block vote' or an overwhelming proportion of it against the 'fanatics, cranks, and extremists' whom Sidney Webb thought largely made up Constituency Party Delegates.

Dr. McKenzie states (without empirical evidence) that Sidney Webb's view was shared by the parliamentary leadership, 'then' and 'now'. Then being in 1930 and now being sometime prior to the publication of his book.[2] He therefore implies that the individual Labour Party member has no real say in the making of policy which is a function exercised *de facto* by the leadership of the PLP.

He even infers that their very resolutions are sabotaged by compositing before they gain the floor of Conference.

> It is sometimes maintained by organisations whose resolutions have been composited into the 'hostile' resolution that it becomes a 'ragbag collection' of propositions which on one ground or another is bound to be unacceptable to most of the delegates. In other words, it is suggested that the Conference Arrangements Committee has skillfully ensured that the omnibus resolutions unacceptable to the Executive are made to look ludicrous in the eyes of the conference by stuffing into them all manner of eccentric views in the Party, with the result that [*sic*] NEC has an easy time in ensuring their defeat.[3]

43

Here, again without real evidence, we are asked to believe that a number of 'fanatics, cranks and extremists' (because they are delegates who wished to move resolutions 'unacceptable to the Executive') would timorously accept as their composite a 'ragbag collection' because a member of the Conference Arrangements Committee is chairman of their compositing meeting.

Somewhat more significant, however, are his figures concerning the fate of resolutions at the 1948, 1949, and 1950 conferences, an analysis of which shows that in 1948 about 40% of all resolutions submitted, including 10 out of 22 composites, were remitted to the NEC without conference discussion; in 1949 the same fate befell nearly 45% of the resolutions including 12 out of 15 composites and in 1950 the figure was 27% of the motions and 8 of 19 composites.[4] No analysis of which organisations were lucky enough to have their motions debated, or whether trade unions fared better or worse than Constituency Parties, is attempted, and, although a very unsatisfactory situation is uncovered, all that is ready established is that a five-day Conference is totally inadequate to deal with an agenda of such proportions.

Professor W. J. M. MacKenzie, in a criticism of Mr. McKenzie's book, thought that his thesis was irrelevant, the Labour Party, he said, is governed under

> . . . the myth of majority decision after full and free discussion. It could not deny the myth without denying its own existence: this is what the Labour Party is [and he thought] . . any shrewd and experienced member of the Labour Party would in private discussion accept Mr. McKenzie's account of how the Party is run.[5]

This has not been proved and I think it is incorrect. Although Dick Crossman in 1956 seemed to agree with McKenzie, who, he said

> . . . has shown conclusively that the two great parties have developed in accordance with the law of increasing oligarchy . . . . power has been concentrated in fewer and fewer hands. The individual party member, . . . now exerts very little effective control over the Party managers. The two big parties are in danger of becoming Party Oligarchies.[6]

But then, McKenzie himself reports that in 1961, ". . . the Chairman of the NEC, R. H. S. Crossman, could write, . . . that it was clear that 'the extra-parliamentary party . . . (is) the final authority on policy issues. . . . "[7]

In any case two other people who were 'shrewd and experienced party members' certainly did not agree. Saul Rose, in fact, conclusively proved that the relationship between the PLP, the NEC and the trade unions during the 3 years when he was employed as secretary of the International Department at Transport House (1952–5) was by no means one of domination of the NEC by the leadership of the PLP. In addition to the evidence he produced to show that though the PLP during this time had the numerical strength, the leadership never had an effective majority owing to the opposition of the Bevanite group of 6 out of 17 MPs who were part of the 27-strong NEC, he also quoted Atlee's letter to Churchill concerning the Laski episode which emphasises the PLP's complete discretion in its conduct of parliamentary business within limits laid down by the Conference. And, he further pointed out that ". . . to attribute NEC majorities at Conference to the consistent backing of the big unions is a superficial and partial analysis". It was the object of the NEC on which the trade unions had representation, to try to define the majority view and to secure a majority. The Annual Conference was the higher authority because it determines the bounds of PLP action.[8]

Robert McKenzie's answer was that Rose had dealt with 1952/5. "I was concerned almost exclusively with the period 1900–1951." But he maintained that the way in which the NEC acted during the time Rose had written about, bore out his contention that the Party's 'ramshackle constitution' was exploited by irresponsible or ambitious rebels and that they had done the Party great damage. 'Why', he asked, "should a few Party activists numbering at most 130,000, in effect, constitute a higher authority than the people elected by 13 million voters?" "What theory of democracy requires that they should be subject to policy decisions or directives issued by the Annual Conference of their Party supporters outside Parliament?"[9]

Mr. Ralph Miliband, who was the other 'shrewd and experienced' party member, pointed out that

> There is precious little evidence for the view that conference delegates both from constituencies and the unions, do not in fact provide a fair cross section of Party opinion. . . . Secondly the undoubted fact that only a minority of registered members of the Labour Party do take an active part in the management of its affairs is certainly deplorable; but the situation is hardly likely to be improved by curtailing what powers the rank and file now have. And thirdly it is surely an odd notion of democracy that the active minority should be penalised for the apathy of the majority.[10]

What has been denied by the leadership is the right of the Annual Conference to lay down the exact priorities which the PLP or a Labour Government should adopt, and *not** the right of conference to lay down binding policy for the movement as a whole.[11]

In that dialogue between leaders and followers which is the essence of democracy in the age of mass politics, Labour Conferences have usually accorded the last word to the Party leaders. But, intra-party democracy at least ensures that there is a dialogue.[12]

This last, along with Rose's view that Conference sets the bounds of PLP action, requires further examination. When a Labour Government is in power, the Prime Minister and the Cabinet (not necessarily in agreement) have been known, as in 1969 with the introduction of the White Paper *In Place of Strife*, to introduce policy which has not been laid down by Conference and parts of which — the penal clauses affecting trade unionists — if they had been laid before it, would certainly have been repudiated by the trade unions and very likely by the constituency parties also. There was no violent CLP reaction to the threat by PLP members that they would refuse to vote for the legislation, and this shows that the extra-parliamentary party can influence the PLP.

Rose's charge that McKenzie's was a partial analysis is, of course, correct, there are only two occasions on which it has been shown that a majority of trade union votes was different to a majority of CLP votes and these were in 1954 when according to Martin Harrison in his book *Trade Unions and The Labour Party Since 1945*, p. 229, the NEC in the debate on German Re-armament won only 24% of the constituency vote,[13] and in 1960 when according to Keith Hindell and Phillip Williams in their article "Scarborough and Blackpool", 67% of CLP votes were cast against unilateralism.[14]

Thus 1954 is the only occasion when support for McKenzie's thesis has been factually demonstrated.

The CND crisis of 1960/61 has been depicted by Dr. McKenzie and others as showing a courageous Hugh Gaitskell defying the Party Conference and refusing to accept its ruling. But Harold Wilson seemed to think that the confrontation need not have assumed the high emotional overtones which it did.[15] In any case it reversed and killed stone dead

*The italics of the original writer.

McKenzie's idea of a ruling alliance of PLP leadership, NEC and the big trade unions walking rough shod over the CLPs. Here were the majority of the CLPs voting with the leadership in 1960 against a majority of trade union votes.

McKenzie also claims that Gaitskell, after fighting off Harold Wilson's challenge for the leadership in November 1960 by 166 votes to 81, took this as a "mandate to defy the Conference".[16]

This of course is not so, Gaitskell did not defy the Conference because constitutionally the motion need not go into the Party Programme. It was lamentably short of a two-thirds majority and Gaitskell was constitutionally within his rights to campaign for its reversal at the next Conference. He would have been equally within his rights to campaign for its reversal even if it had gained the necessary majority, but he could not have stopped it going into the Party Programme and the battle then would probably have been joined on whether it should go into a Manifesto.

Dr. McKenzie raises the question first raised he says by Leon Epstein in an article entitled "Who makes Party Policy: British Labour 1960—61". Whether the PLP could have ignored a second decision in favour of unilaterialism if the 1961 conference had failed to reverse itself. The evidence, he says, "suggests that Gaitskell and a majority of the PLP had no intention of accepting direction from its conference and they therefore defied the 1961 resolutions as flatly as they had those of 1960". The resolutions he refers to are the one demanding the removal of the 'Polaris' base from Britain and the one objecting to the training of German troops here. McKenzie says "But again Gaitskell and the PLP refused to be bound by either resolution and they made no move to advocate these policies in parliament."[17]

What he does not say, of course, is that neither of these motions got a two-thirds majority either. He does not state what the evidence is and I think it much more likely that if the Conference had stayed unilaterialist by a large majority that Gaitskell would have been forced to accept it, as he had been forced to abandon his attempt to change Clause IV in 1959/60, but that he would have tried to modify and emasculate it. The alternative would have been to isolate himself as the main factor of disunity. Even McKenzie admits that if the Parliamentary Party remained at odds with its Party Conference on matters of major policy, ". . . the likely consequence would be the break up of the Party".[18]

People have been predicting the break up of the Party because of the wide range of views within it on which policies provide the best and quickest road to democratic socialism, since its inception. If the views were permanently polarised into a clear division of right and left, break up would be inevitable. But right and left are shifting qualities for most party members. Some no doubt adjust their views on all policy items to coincide with the views expressed by the people with whom they wish to identify, but my experience of most Labour Party members is that they like to make up their minds and express their views separately on separate issues.

Of course Labour Party members complain about the non-implementation of resolutions which Conference has passed and about the disappearance of those remitted to the NEC. Resolutions on this subject appear with great regularity on the Conference Agenda, often couched in very belligerent terms. Such a motion, Composite 16, was discussed at the 1970 Conference.

> This Conference believes that the PLP leaders, whether in government or opposition, should reflect the views and aspirations of the Labour Party and Trade Union Movement by framing their policies on Annual Conference decisions.
> While appreciating that the Parliamentary Labour Party must deal with matters arising in Parliament which have not been the subject of Annual Conference decision, it deplores the PLP's refusal to act on Conference decisions.

This was moved by Mr. C. Muir of Manchester Exchange who said

> we have been brought up to know that we can voice our views and opinions at Ward meetings, take them forward for discussion at Divisional meetings or on the shop floor via the branch meeting through our trade union and finally have them discussed at annual conference, to be approved or turned down as our policies. This is Democracy. . . . It has been stated that when Labour is in opposition the Parliamentary leadership should observe conference decisions but when the Party is in government the Cabinet can ignore them. This I believe is unacceptable, as indeed it was to Henderson, to Lansbury and to Atlee in the past, . . . Why have we lost 150,000 Party members since being returned to government in 1964.

The delegate then cited the reintroduction of prescription charges, the Labour Governments' failure to achieve higher economic growth, its refusal to dissociate itself from American policy in Vietnam, the introduction of a wage freeze, and a reference to *In Place of Strife.*[19] The seconder of the motion said: "... in no way does it tie the hands of the Parliamentary Labour Party, or indeed the next Labour Government, in the timing of legislation based on agreed policy."[20] And a very significant speech was made by Mrs. Margaret McCarthy* the delegate from Oxford CLP who said:

> ...nobody in this hall is stupid enough to think that conference can determine day to day decisions of the Parliamentary Party when they are in office ... everybody in this room operates this system. Constituency Parties very well understand the relationship between Labour Groups and GMCs. We operate that system. If we are Trade Union Delegates we understand the relationship between our Annual Conference decisions and the day to day work of the Executive Committee and full time officers of the Union. They operate those systems every day of their lives. So we are not asking that we should cross every t and dot every i for the Parliamentary Labour Party. What effectively we are saying is that unless we are given greater participation in the decision making of this Party's policy, then we have become meaningless as a Party – we no longer exist. ... We are asking that the broad outlines of Party policy should be determined here. I suggest that in addition it is reasonable that we should ask when it proves impossible, for reasons outside either Party or Labour Government control, to implement these, that we should be given a reasonable explanation of why it has proved impossible. I think what we all resent most is, not that decisions have not been carried out, but that we have been treated with a [sic] cynicism in the rejection of conference decisions–."[21]

Harold Wilson, replying for the Executive, asked for the motion to be remitted to the NEC because under the terms on an NEC statement accepted by Conference almost unanimously the same morning "... calls for further thought about the relationship between the NEC, Annual Conference and the Parliamentary Labour Party, whether in government or opposition, and we intend this to lead to the greater participation for which the last speaker asked",[22] The resolution was carried against the NEC recommendation.[23]

Professor MacKenzie believes the Labour Party operates under "... the myth of majority decision following full and frank discussion". Yet, here were delegates who were perfectly aware of the constitutional position, who knew that the Labour Government had acted constitutionally correctly but who thought it *ought* to have acted otherwise on these items

*Now Lady McCarthy.

and were exercising their democratic right to say so. They were asking for greater participation and for consultation and explanation if the leadership did not or could not meet conferences' wishes. And, the leader of the Party assured them that the NEC was already considering this matter with a view to providing for increased participation. The conference nevertheless still voted against the leader's recommendation. The issues complained of constituted a small fraction of the legislation carried through with conference approval during the 6 years in office of the Labour Government. There is nothing mythical about this process. But the call for greater membership participation in decisions regarding the implementation of policy raises the question of Oligarchy.

Oligarchy or Democracy

Lipsett, Trow and Coleman, "Democracy and Oligarchy in Trade Unions", set out to prove that an institutional opposition such as that in the International Typographical Union of America, coupled with a high rate of turnover of the top leadership, nationally and locally, is a prerequisite for democratic status in any voluntary organisation. The authors give no details of the re-election of defeated personnel, or the existence of any significant policy differences. Neither do they give any indication of the proportion of the electorate who participate in union elections.[24]

As John Hughes in a research paper says: Their

> advocacy does not proceed from any general *Justification* of the identification of democratic processes in unions primarily with the existence of organised opposition(s). It is clear that the existence of such an organised struggle becomes used as if it were an index of the extent of democracy. But the identification is merely *asserted* rather than argued.[25]

Roderick Martin, "Union Democracy: an Explanatory Framework", argues that the toleration of opposing factions and not the turnover of leaders is the prime indication of democracy in unions.

> The survival of faction limits executive ability to disregard rank and file opinion by providing the *potential* means for its overthrow (although the potential is rarely realised). Faction is an indispensible sanction against leadership failure to respond to membership opinion.[26]

The Labour Party has a massive toleration of internal factions on a multiplicity of subjects which are themselves either dissipated or concentrated in the broad shifting factions of right and left. Specific and intense factions like CND can raise controversy resembling civil war, but the Party survives.

Robert Michels 'Iron Law of Oligarchy' holds that leadership groups in voluntary socialist societies become impervious to opposition from below, due to the authority building nature of organisation. "Who says organisation says Oligarchy" is quoted by all who examine the structure and functions of voluntary socialist organisations with a view to assessing the democratic content. An immunity to challenge is developed through the mass membership need for the co-ordinating functions of leaders who acquire and hoard specialised knowledge in an attempt to promote their own indispensability.

Michels really thought of democracy in terms of Rousseau's 'true democracy', i.e. total participation entailing the circulation of governmental positions and duties among the entire citizenship. But Rousseau said that a 'true democracy' had never existed and never will. In a large or complex state where the whole assembly cannot assemble to govern at all times, 'true democracy' is not only impossible but also inappropriate and undesirable.

> . . . for things which ought to be kept apart are not. . . . It is not good that he who makes the law should execute it or that the body of the people should turn its attention away from general perspectives and give it to particular objects.[27]

> If it were possible for the sovereign, . . . to have the executive power, then the de jure and the de facto would be so confused that people, would no longer know what was law and what was not.[28]

Any mass membership organisation which functions under a 'general will' must therefore elect a governing body under rules laid down in its constitution and if this is an elective aristocracy, frequently elected, with a large turnover of delegates who are not, and could not be, representatives; they are merely agents;[29] as in the British Labour Party, then the society may qualify as a democracy conforming to Rousseau's more practical use of the word.

P. W. Medding, "Power in Political Parties", points out that

> Michels nowhere took note of the internal organisation and structural consequences of associational voluntariness, political competition and the need to maximise public support, namely that limitations will be exercised over leaders by followers.[30]

Withdrawal of support by ordinary branch members or the PLP can be a very effective limitation.

Furthermore, even Dr. McKenzie agrees that the 'Law of Oligarchy' is not 'iron' because leaders in British political parties are both opposed and displaced by followers, although he believes more evidence for this exists pertaining to the Tory than the Labour Party.[31]   I would dispute this; Macdonald and Lansbury were both displaced, Atlee was careful to defer to the wishes of Annual Conference, Gaitskell retreated in the face of the Clause IV storm and it is not possible to be categorical about him in 1960/61 if his opponents had mustered a majority large enough to give them constitutional backing. Furthermore, he *was* challenged for the leadership by Harold Wilson, who in 1969 had in his turn to retreat from his entrenched position on *In Place of Strife*, and refusal to do so might have cost him both government and leadership.

The question also arises — who is the leadership?, certainly regarding the implementation of policy. A Labour Cabinet is by no means always at one, the leader and deputy leader are often poles apart regarding policy issues. George Brown and Roy Jenkins, two powerful deputy leaders, both resigned because of disagreements on policy and Michels' view that resignations are tendered merely to strengthen the resigners' position cannot be upheld in either case. Certainly not in the case of George Brown who resigned himself out of the Party leadership in a very effective and permanent way. Furthermore, Harold Wilson resigned as both Prime Minister and Leader without dispute or discernible reason other than that he felt he had served long enough, which surely destroys any suggestion that the Party Leadership or the government of the Party is a self-perpetuating Oligarchy.

References

1. *Op. cit.*, McKenzie, p. 626.
2. *Ibid.*, p. 505.

3. *Ibid.*, p. 495.
4. *Ibid.*, p. 496.
5. MacKenzie, W. J. M., "Mr. McKenzie on the British Parties", *Political Studies*, Vol. 3 (1955) p. 157.
6. Crossman, R. H. S., *Socialism and the New Despotism*, Fabian Tract 298 (1956), p. 21.
7. *Op. cit.*, McKenzie, p. 626.
8. Rose, Saul, "Policy Decision in Opposition", *Political Studies*, Vol. 4 (1956) p. 128 ff.
9. McKenzie, Robert T., "Policy Decision in Opposition a Rejoiner", *Political Studies*, Vol. 5 (1976) pp. 176 ff.
10. Miliband, Ralph, "Democracy and Parliamentary Government", *Political Studies*, Vol. 6 (1958) p. 170.
11. *Ibid.*, p. 171.
12. *Ibid.*, p. 173.
13. *Op cit.*, McKenzie, *British Political Parties*, p. 61n.
14. Hindell, Keith and Phillip, Williams, "Scarborough & Blackpool", *Political Quarterly*, Vol. 33, No. 3, pp. 306 ff.
15. *Op. cit.*, McKenzie, *British Political Parties*, p. 621.
16. *Ibid.*, p. 622.
17. *Ibid.*, p. 624,
18. *Ibid.*, p. 624.
19. *The Labour Party Annual Report 1970*, pp. 180 and 181.
20. *Ibid.*, p. 181.
21. *Ibid.*, pp. 182 and 183.
22. *Ibid.*, p. 183.
23. *Ibid.*, p. 185.
24. Lipset, S. M., Trow, M. A. and Coleman, J. S., "Democracy & Oligarchy in Trade Unions" (1956), *Trade Unions* (ed.) W. E. J. McCarthy (1972), pp. 155 ff.
25. Hughes, John D., "Should Party Systems be Encouraged in Trade Unions? The Case of The British Communist Party" (1967), *Trade Unions* (ed.) W. E. J. McCarthy (1972), p. 173.
26. Martin, Roderick, "Union Democracy: an Exploratory Framework" (1968), *Trade Unions* (ed.) W. E. J. McCarthy (1972), pp. 191 and 192.
27. *Op. cit.*, Rousseau, Bk. III, Chap. 4, p. 112.
28. *Ibid.*, Bk. III, Chap. 16, p. 144.
29. *Ibid.*, Bk. III, Chap. 15, p. 141.
30. *Op. cit.*, Medding, p. 2.
31. *Op cit.*, McKenzie, *British Political Parties*, p. 644.

CHAPTER 8

Conclusions

In Chapter 1 I introduced my subject and outlined my method of approach. In Chapter 2 I examined the democratic theories of J. J. Rousseau, G. D. H. Cole and J. S. Mill and found that while each approached the concept of government from a different standpoint, a common factor united them all. Each desired that his citizens should take part in some aspects of the governmental functions which affected their lives. Rousseau wished his people to accept, interpret and express the 'General Will' which would teach them to think and act in respect of themselves and each other and this dependence on the law and on each other would give them a moral code and a sense of identity and security.

Cole wanted his guildsman to have some control over all the interests which might affect him so that he would feel integrated into his environment and be able to work to improve it for himself and others.

Mill wanted his people to improve their lot gradually so that no one suffered from the ambitions of others.

Each was concerned to educate his polity, both morally by encouraging people to identify with others through working together in matters of mutual concern, and practically through the acquisition of specialised knowledge which only the performance of a function may provide.

Participation therefore meant personal identification, integration, a sense of civic security and moral and functional education.

In Chapter 3 I examined the Labour Party as an entity and noted its close analogy to Rousseau's Republic and the high degree of participation which is possible in the governmental processes within it. The membership share in the sovereignty and accept the 'General Will' enshrined in its constitution. The leadership has a built-in autonomy which protects the Party from the danger of Ochlocracy which might result, if the Party government, which is an elective aristocracy with a high degree of membership participation due to frequent elections (yearly) and a constant interchange of delegates, were to insist on dangerous or impossible policies owing to misdirection or ignorance. That is not to say, that this automony is never abused.

The participatory process in the Labour Party is very educational because of the complexity of issues with which delegates, workers and administrative representatives become involved, especially as each one may have a direct influence in the decisions which finally become law. The process is also very integrative, there is a great sense of 'belonging' among Labour Party members and this gives it a self-sustaining character.

Rousseau would not have accepted the Labour Party as a 'true democracy' but Labour Party members are not 'gods' and it is quite obviously and manifestly, a democracy in his more practical use of the term.

In Chapter 4 I have shown that democratic, elective aristocracy also governs the Party at its local levels in Branches and parent CLPs. The elections are frequent and the officers and delegates are subject to yearly change.

The federal structure of the Party allows the multiplicity of representation which is clearly analogous to Cole's 'ideal' form of self-government in an industrial consumer society. This provides functional representation giving direct and indirect transmission of information. It gives the participant separate domestic, social, industrial and political identities which are each integrative in their own sphere, which promote a physical and moral awareness of the needs of others and which combine to give the member an organisational as well as a personal identity.

Those members who accept the system are willing to maintain it and help to make it work by carrying out the everyday basic jobs which ensure its continued existence, i.e. election work, fund raising, etc., without wishing to involve themselves in its governmental functions, demonstrate Mill's concept of participation which is educational, useful, self-sacrificing by helping others, through promoting the polity's essential purpose, and which therefore is both integrative and self-sustaining.

In Chapter 5 I have dealt with the Women's Movement which performs mainly an advisory, supportive and educational service to the Party. It provides an extra avenue of representation for those women who are able and wish to use it, but comparatively few women in the Party utilise their constitutional equality by becoming involved in the higher levels of party governmental activity even in spite of enabling dispensations to CLPs to appoint extra women delegates to Annual Conference. The majority of female members concentrate their activities on participation in the work of their Branch or women's section or both, and therefore enjoy the educational and other benefits of this. The women's movement makes a significant contribution to the level of political awareness and intelligence within the Party. It is internally self-governing in the democratically elective way which is common to Party institutions. Its members are well integrated and for the most part seem content with the participatory supportive functions in which it excels. It demonstrates all the advantages of internal participatory democracy and can be closely identified with Mill's ideas.

In Chapter 6 I have shown that the Youth movement has been fragmentary, but it has not, until the Simpson Report, been allowed the responsibility of self-government above Branch level. I believe this may have contributed to its instability.

The movement has nevertheless made significant contributions to the Party, especially at local level where branches were often sufficiently self-sustaining to weather all of the national storms.

The Party has benefited in man and woman power from the educational and other advantages of an influx of membership from the Youth movement because of the effects of its advisory, educational, recreational and participatory purposes.

The movement has, because of a paternalistic reluctance by the government of the Party to grant it internal sovereignty, been the least democratic of the Party institutions, but the enabling recommendations of the Simpson Committee have given it a constitution which now enables it to function as a democratic organ within a democratic polity.

In Chapter 7 I have examined some of the complaints which seek to deny or modify the Labour Party's claim of intra-party democracy. The complaints were:

1. That the leadership of the PLP dominates the NEC and forms a conspiracy with the large trade unions to frustrate CLP resolutions; by

(a) combining to outmanoeuvre or outvote them,

(b) by the PLP/NEC refusing to implement policy when it is passed.

The only factual evidence concerning (a) is contradictory. In 1954 the trade unions outvoted the CLPs who voted against the leadership and lost.

But in 1960 the trade unions outvoted the CLPs who voted with the leadership and still lost.

Furthermore, Ralph Miliband points out that there is a paucity of evidence suggesting that conference delegates across the board, do not constitute a fair cross section of views on Party policy.

On (b) Saul Rose provides direct evidence that during his term of office at Transport House, the PLP did not control the NEC.

2. Alternatively McKenzie argues that a responsible PLP should not have to answer to an unrepresentative number of Party activists.

Miliband points out that these are the only people in an age of mass politics who ensure that *any* dialogue on policy takes place.

3. Resolutions are improperly treated:
(a) by Conference Arrangements Committee, I think I have established that this is arrant nonsense, and
(b) by remission through not being reached. This is a valid complaint which needs attention (see below, p. 59).

4. Intra-Party democracy is a myth. This is resoundingly refuted by the debate on Composite 16 at the 1970 Annual Conference especially by the contribution of the Oxford delegate. But any debate on this subject at Annual Conferences across the years will show that the delegates were and are aware of the constitutional position.

Finally I discuss Oligarchy and establish that unless the term is so narrowly defined as to be absolutely meaningless, the British Labour Party is not governed by Oligarchy. In fact, my thesis is that the Labour Party may be classified as a highly participatory democratic form of elective aristocracy even under Rousseau's nomenclature and its internal institutions are a close analogy to the ideal polities of Rousseau, Cole and Mill.

The psychological effects on party members, of the educational, integrative and self-sustaining nature of participation in the Party's work and government, emerge as the development of moral codes, political awareness, the development of personal, civil and organisational identities, the promotion of an awareness of the physical and moral needs of others, the desire to work to improve the lot of people generally and to devise policies which will bring about conditions conducive to the promotion of public welfare in social, industrial, moral and intellectual fields.

These are the sort of criteria which Carole Patement has established are required in a participatory democratic polity[1] and in meeting them, I submit, the British Labour Party is in fact, A FUNCTIONING PARTICIPATORY DEMOCRACY.

But, there are two main areas where action needs to be taken to strengthen the participatory abilities of the membership:

1. Only a small number of individual party members participate FULLY, even in their Party Branches. The facilities to enable them to do so are there, but are not taken advantage of. This is classified as apathy, but it could be that the Party has failed to stimulate an interest which was strong enough to bring them into the Party in the first place, which keeps them paying their subscription and which impels a majority of them to give some sort of help during elections. The first knowledge these members obtain of current party policy apart from what they may glean from their newspapers and the communications media, probably comes to them through the election literature which is supplied to them, at the same time and in the same quantity as that which is circulated to the general public.

Literature costs money and there's the rub. What is the point in wasting scarce resources by circulating material which seems to produce no response? But a response could be called for. If CLPs decided to hold primary elections for their prospective candidates among their members. The Branch or CLP could choose a short list and circulate biographical material and a ballot paper to be returned by post or collection on a specific date. The CLP Executive Committee could appoint a returning officer to see that it was run fairly. Such a selection process might well evoke a participatory response.

2. At CLP level the scope for personal participation of ordinary members is widely thought to be adequate although proposals for general meetings of members have been made and some parties, e.g. Oxford CLP, open their management committee meetings to all individual members, who are often allowed to take a full part in the proceedings without voting power which is restricted to delegates.

Above CLP level the situation leaves much to be desired. Regional Conferences may discuss only matters of Regional Policy and in my opinion are of very limited value. Annual Conference refers a large number of the motions submitted to it to the NEC without discussing them. The NEC does consider these but the situation is less than satisfactory. Five days for such a large Conference to cope even in the most cursory way with all the business submitted to it is obviously quite inadequate. Yet, to lengthen the Conference would be to impose unacceptable conditions on the delegates, most of whom have to earn their living, and many of whom are already sacrificing a part of their annual holiday. Furthermore, there is a limit to the length of time that even the most dedicated party member can be expected to remain alert and involved under conference conditions. Neither could a rotation system for submitting resolutions, which would ensure that they would all be dealt with, be devised to operate under the present system. But it is possible that the Regional machinery could be put to some useful purpose here. Inigo Bing in his article "New Approaches to Democracy" has made a similar but less drastic proposal to the following.[2]

An additional Regional Conference, separate to the Regional Annual Meeting for the single purpose of dealing with resolutions for Annual Conference, could be convened in each Region.

CLPs could submit motions to this conference either on a rotation basis, allowing them a resolution, say every third year, or through a grouping of the appropriate number of CLPs, each of which would put forward a group motion annually.

A Regional Conference Arrangements Committee could send a sufficient number of copies of all motions submitted to CLPs to allow them to circulate their Branches.

Parties who had submitted similar motions would be asked to communicate with each other to arrange a suitable composite.

All resolutions or composites would be debated and the one surviving an exhaustive ballot would be submitted for Annual Conference. There would therefore be eleven or possibly twelve CLP motions and these would again be subject to compositing along with motions from trade unions and socialist societies.

Inter-regional composites might be avoided if the Regional Conferences were staggered to allow each to know progressively what the others had submitted.

Annual Conference Arrangements Committee should then try to ensure that all regional motions, especially those which were not to be accepted by the NEC, should be debated. All resolutions whether remitted or accepted by conference should be the subject of a report on action taken on them in the NEC report for the following year.

Motions to change the constitution should be submitted to the NEC without changing the present procedure.

References

1. Pateman, Carole, *op. cit.*, pp. 42 ff.
2. Bing, Inigo, "New Approaches to Democracy", *The Labour Party: an organisation study* (ed.) Inigo Bing, Fabian Tract 407 (1971).

Appendix A

DIAGRAM ILLUSTRATING THE STRUCTURE
OF A CONSTITUENCY LABOUR PARTY

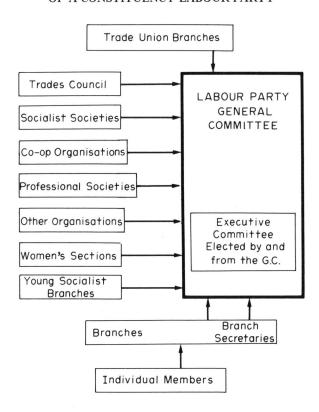

The affiliated societies, branches, women's sections and Young Socialist branches send delegates on a basis to be specified by the constituency party in its rules. The branch secretaries are *ex officio* delegates with voting power.

General Note

Trades Councils are now rarely affiliated; they cannot use industrial funds for political affiliations. The Socialist, professional and other organisations may overlap.

Party Organisation (1975)

Appendix B

DIAGRAM ILLUSTRATING THE STRUCTURE
OF A COUNTY PARTY
(Regional Party in Scotland)

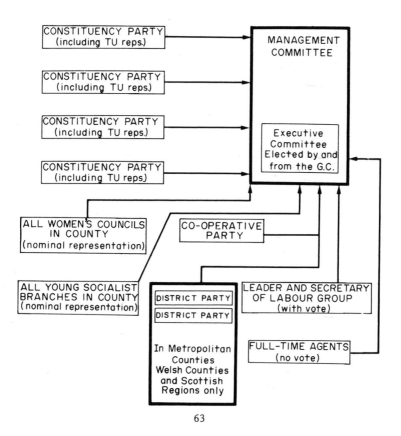

Note: Representation to the Management Committee from each Constituency to include representatives of Trade Union and Socialist Societies affiliated to that Constituency Party.

General Note

No diagrams have been included for District Parties as these operate under a variety of structures.

Party Organisation (1975)

Appendix C

RULES FOR GREATER LONDON BOROUGHS AND CONSTITUENCIES

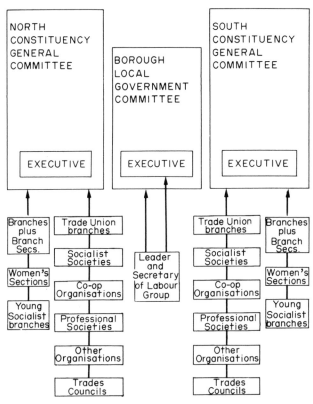

Note: Representation to the Local Government Committee from each Constituency to include the Constituency Chairman and Secretary

and representatives of the various groups of organisations affiliated
to that Constituency Party.

Party Organisation (1975)

Appendix D

THE LABOUR PARTY
NATIONAL LABOUR WOMEN'S ADVISORY COMMITTEE
February 1971

	Women candidates					
Year	Conservative	Labour	Liberal	Others	Total elected	Total no. of women candidates
1918	1	4	4	8(1)*	1	17
1922	5(1)	10	16(1)	2	2	33
1923	7(3)	14(3)	12(2)	1	8	34
1924	12(3)	22(1)	6	1	4	41
1929	10(3)	30(9)	25(1)	4(1)	14	69
1931	17(13)	36	5(1)	4(1)	15	62
1935	19(6)	33(1) 2 ILP	11(1)	2(1)	9	67
1945	14(1) 1 Ind. Con.	41(21)	20(1)	11(1)	24	87
1950	28(6)	42(14)	45(1)	11	21	126
1951	25(6)	41(11)	11	–	17	77
1953	33(10)	43(14)	14	2	24	92
1959	28(12)	36(13)	16	1	25	81
1964	23(11)	33(18)	25	8	29	89
1966	21(7)	30(19)	20	9	26	80
1970	26(15)	29(10)	23	21(1)	26	99
Feb. 1974	33(9)	40(13)	40	30(1)	23	143 } †
Oct. 1974	30(7)	50(18)	49	32(2)	27	161 } †

*One successful – Countess Markieviez – Irish Nationalist who did not take her seat.

Viscountess Astor (Cons.), elected in 1919 in a by-election, was the first woman to sit in the House of Commons.

Figures in brackets denote number of Candidates elected for each Party.

NAD/W/12/2/71
†These figures have been added to the original document.

67

Appendix E

Hon. Sec.,
Rt. Hon. A. Henderson M.P.,
Acting Secretary,
J. S. Middleton,
National Agent,
Egerton P. Ware.

THE LABOUR PARTY

The Labour Party,
33 Eccleston Square,
London SW1.

Organisation of Youth
August 1924

To the Labour Parties in the Constituencies

Dear Secretary,

As you are aware the Executive Committee of the Labour Party appointed a Sub-Committee to consider the question of the Organisation of Youth, and a Questionnaire was sent out to all the Labour Parties throughout the country asking for information as to present activities in that direction and their views as to whether efforts should be made for the organisation of young people as a part of the ordinary activities of the Labour Party. In a very large majority of cases the replies were emphatically in favour of this work, and the Executive Committee adopted a report from the Sub-Committee recommending that the

ORGANISATION OF YOUNG PEOPLE

should become part of the ordinary organising work of the Party, in order that they should more readily and enthusiastically take their place in the Labour Movement as they reach adult years. In order to carry out this purpose and also to avoid multiplication of organisations and efforts, the Committee feel that it is very important that Young People's Sections should be part of the organisation in the constituencies and not part of separate national organisations, and in the following recommendations they suggest a scheme which can be put into operation and which will require no alteration in the constitution of the Party and yet will give to the young people the right means of co-operating in the general work of the constituencies, without forcing upon them responsibilities and duties which should only be borne by the organisations of adult members in the Party. It is therefore proposed that in establishing

YOUNG PEOPLE'S SECTIONS

the following scheme should be adopted:—

1. That Young People's Sections should be formed which shall be attached to and form part of the Local Labour Parties.

2. That boys and girls between the ages of 14 and 21 shall be eligible for membership.

3. That the minimum subscription shall be 6d. per year.

4. That the Young People's Section shall be governed by a Committee of Management and officers elected by the Section from amongst its own members, together with at least two persons appointed by the General Committee of the Labour Party.

5. That the Young People's Section should appoint two of its members to represent it on the General Committee of the Local Labour Party, both of whom shall be over 16 years of age and who shall have power to take part in the proceedings but not to vote.

While it is proposed that the minimum age shall be 14 the Committee desire to make it clear that they do not in any way discourage the formation of

JUNIOR SECTIONS FOR CHILDREN

under 14 mainly on a recreational character, but they think it is unnecessary to lay down any special plans for bringing these into contact with the political side of the Movement. For children below the age of 14 they deprecate the teaching of political doctrines, and they do not think that children at these early years should have any place even as non-voting members in the governing bodies of the Parties. For the older boys and girls they think it is important that they should have as much autonomy as possible, but the appointment of two members by the General Committee on the

COMMITTEE OF MANAGEMENT

of the Young People's Section would enable the work of the young people to be closer co-ordinated with that of the Party and also would enable the young members to have the guidance of people more experienced in the Party's work. In general it will probably be found best that at least one of these members should be the Secretary of the Local Labour Party and one should be a member of the Women's Section. It is felt to be important that the representation of the Young People's Section on the General Committee should not be the full representation given to the Men's and Women's Sections. If the young people were to be given voting power and be placed in the same position as these other Sections they might be used as a field for exploitation by either side whenever disagreement existed in the Party, and they might even be put in the position in a matter for example of the selection of candidates of having the final decision in their hands. Under the method suggested close contact may be maintained without putting young boys and girls in a position which their experience would not entitle them to take and which those who are still considered even by the Labour Party too young to vote for Parliament and other public bodies ought not to have. At the same time those members of Young People's Sections who desire to have the full power of individual members may if they are old enough join the Men's and Women's Sections and exercise their rights there. No age limit has been laid down in the Labour Party Constitution, but it is customary to take individual members from the age of 16 though not younger.

The work of the Young People's Sections should be mainly

RECREATIONAL AND EDUCATIONAL

and care should be taken not to over-emphasize their political side. In organising their work the attitude of the Labour Party should be one of encouragement and help in all developments which the young people are keen to follow. Three main lines are suggested:—

1. Recreational. Opportunity should be found for sports, music, dramatic societies and social intercourse.

2. Educational. All developments should be encouraged in the way of study circles, classes, debates, an understanding of the conduct of public work, and all of these should be conducted in association with the Local Labour Party.

3. Participation in Election Work. Every encouragement should be given for this and full advantage taken of the young people's energy and desire to serve.

In addition to the Young People's Sections, Junior Sections of children up to 14 may find a place in the work. In developing these the help of the Women's Section is specially valuable, and with the growth of the Young People's Sections many of the boys and girls will also be able to give assistance with the younger children. For them, singing, dancing, dramatic societies, sports and gymnastics, should play the greater part but they can also get useful training by helping in the conduct of their own meetings as Chairman, Secretaries, etc.

The Executive Committee hope that the

LOCAL LABOUR PARTIES

will be able to take up this matter with energy and enthusiasm, for it is important that we should realise that association with the Labour Movement may well begin amongst growing boys and girls. The boys already become responsible citizens at 21, and we hope that very soon the same will be the case with the girls. The period between school time and adult life is one during which little provision is made for the young people to develop their interests in questions of citizenship, and if developed upon proper lines the Young People's Sections would prove an invaluable organisation for the creation of that educated democracy upon which the success of Labour must depend.

We shall be very glad if you will bring this subject at an early date before your Committee and let us know whether you are able to take action upon the lines suggested.

I am,

Yours very truly,

EGERTON P. WAKE,

National Agent.

Appendix F

ANDY BEVAN

In August 1976 a meeting comprising three members of the NEC Sub-Committee for Staff Negotiations voted 2 to 1 in favour of appointing Mr. Andy Bevan the 24-year-old National Chairman of the Labour Party Young Socialists who is a self-acclaimed Trotskyist and supporter of the Militant Group* as the Labour Party's National Youth Officer at a salary of £4000 per year.

The decision was ratified by a meeting of the NEC at Blackpool on Friday 24 September.

On Sunday, 26 September the Annual Meeting of the National Union of Labour Organisers decided unanimously to ask the NEC to annul the appointment and instructed its membership, including Ron Hayward the General Secretary of the Party and Reg Underhill the National Agent, not to co-operate with Mr. Bevan in any way. The reason for this was that the post had previously been filled, except on one occasion when Mr. Alan Lee Williams, a member of the Transport and General Workers' Union had held it (see p. 38), by a member of NULO, and it seemed unfair to the union that the post should now fall to an outsider. Joint meetings between NULO and the National Party Officers were held on 5 and 18 October and on 10 November, but the situation remained unaltered.

The Prime Minister Rt. Hon. James Callaghan M.P. wrote to the NEC asking that the appointment be rescinded because he did not think Mr. Bevan would be able to act in the politically neutral way appropriate to the paid Officers of the National Party and on Tuesday, 23 November the

*The Militant Group are a number of left wing party members, many of them calling themselves Trotskyites, who support and promote the policies and ideas of the weekly newspaper *Militant*.

NEC postponed further action for one month because a Cabinet meeting had prevented some NEC members attending and in order to enable negotiations between NULO and the Party Officers to continue.

On Monday, 20 December a meeting comprising representatives of NULO and a Sub-Committee of the NEC decided that an appeal to remove the boycott on Mr. Bevan would be made to a full meeting of NULO members early in 1977. This meeting was held on Monday, 10 January 1977 when NULO once again instructed its members not to co-operate with Mr. Bevan and refused to accept him as a member.

Mr. Bevan reported for work at Transport House on Tuesday, 11 January but was sent home by the General Secretary. The following day the General Secretary and the Labour Party Chairman Mr. John Chalmers met a NULO delegation led by Mr. Arthur Clare, General Secretary of NULO, and invited NULO representatives to address the NEC at its next meeting on Wednesday, 19 January, at which the NEC voted 18 – nil to confirm the appointment of Mr. Bevan as National Youth Officer. But the Union was offered a joint working party to look into the grievances that lay behind the dispute and although Mr. Bevan continued to hold the position, organisational posts in the future would be offered in the first instance to NULO members.

NULO quite clearly had a very good case and on custom and practice alone the job in the first instance should have been offered to their members.

It is nevertheless fortunate that having once confirmed the appointment, the NEC upheld it, and that the National Officers finally agreed to work with Mr. Bevan, because, although the post is organisational and therefore filled by NEC appointment and not Youth Movement election, and although the Labour Party Young Socialists are by no means 'militant dominated', a decision to renege could have had a very damaging effect, would undoubtedly have been a great setback for the Youth Movement and would very likely have destroyed the abilities for self-government in the movement brought about by the Simpson recommendations.

Bibliography

Benn, Anthony W., *the new politics a socialist reconnaissance*, Fabian Tract 402 (1970).

Benn, S. I. and Peters, R. S., *Social Principles and the Democratic State*, George Allen & Unwin Ltd., London (1959).

Berry, Ralph, *How to Write a Research Paper*, Pergamon Press (1966).

Bing, Inigo, "New Approaches to Democracy", *The Labour Party: an organisational study* (ed.) Inigo Bing, Fabian Tract 407 (1971), p. 20.

Cole, G. D. H., *Guild Socialism Re-stated*, George Allen & Unwin Ltd. (1920).

Cole, G. D. H., *A History of the Labour Party from 1914*, Routledge & Kegan Paul Ltd., London (1948).

Cole, G. D. H., *The National Coal Board*, Fabian Pamphlet (1948).

Crossman, Rt. Hon. R. H. S., MP, *Socialism and the New Despotism*, Fabian Tract 298 (1956).

Hindell, Keith and Williams, Phillip, "Scarborough & Blackpool", *Political Quarterly*, Vol. 33, No. 3.

Hughes, John, "Should Party Systems be Encouraged in Trade Unions? The Case of the British Communist Party" (1967), *Trade Unions* (ed.) W. E. J. McCarthy, Penguin Books Ltd. (1972), p. 172.

Jupp, J., *Political Parties*, Routledge & Kegan Paul Ltd. (1968).

Lipset, S. M., Trow, M. A. and Coleman, J. S., "Democracy & Oligarchy in Trade Unions", *Trade Unions* (ed.) W. E. J. McCarthy, Penguin Books Ltd. (1972), p. 155.

MacKenzie, W. J. M., "Mr. McKenzie on British Politics", *Political Studies*, Vol. 3 (1955).

McKenzie, R. T., *British Political Parties*, Heinemann, London (1964).

McKenzie, R. T., "Policy Decision in Opposition a Rejoiner", *Political Studies*, Vol. 5 (1957).

Martin, Roderick, "Union Democracy: an Explanatory Framework" (1968), *Trade Unions* (ed.) W. E. J. McCarthy, Penguin Books Ltd. (1972).

Medding, P. V., "Power in Political Parties", *Political Studies*, No. 18, p. 1.

Michels, Robert, *Political Parties*, trans. Eden and Cedar Paul, Dover Publications Inc., New York (1959), Constable & Co. Ltd., London.

Miliband, Ralph, "Democracy and Parliamentary Government", *Political Studies*, Vol. 6 (1958).

Mill, John, S., *Utilitarianism, Liberty and Representative Government*, Everyman (1910).

Pateman, Carole, *Participation and Democratic Theory*, Cambridge U.P. (1970).

Pelling, Henry, *Origins of the Labour Party*, Oxford Paperback (1965).

Phillips, Morgan, *Constitution of the Labour Party*, The Labour Party (1960).

Pickles, Dorothy, *Democracy*, B. T. Batsford Ltd., London (1970).
Poirier, Philip P., *The Advent of the Labour Party*, George Allen & Unwin Ltd. (1958).
Rose, Saul, "Policy Decision in Opposition", *Political Studies*, Vol. 4 (1956).
Rousseau, Jean J., *The Social Contract*, trans. Maurice Cranston, Penguin Books Ltd. (1968).
Sanderson Furniss, Averil, D., "The Citizenship of Women", *The Book of the Labour Party* (ed.) Herbert Tracey, Caxton Publishing Co. Ltd. (1925), Vol. II, p. 258.
Talmon, J. L., *The Origins of Totalitarian Democracy*, Secker & Warbury (1955).
Tracey, Herbert (ed.), *The Book of the Labour Party*, Vols. I, II and III. Caxton Publishing Co. Ltd., London (1952).
Wayper, C. L., *Political Thought*, Teach Yourself Books (1954).
Webb, Beatrice, *Our Partnership* (eds.) Barbara Drake and M. Cole (1948), Longman, Green & Co. (London) (1948).
Webb, S. and Webb, B., *The History of Trade Unionism, 1666–1920*, printed by the Authors for the Trade Unionists of the United Kingdom, Christmas 1919.
Whitaker, Ben, *participation and poverty*, Fabian Research Series 272 (1968).
Wilson, Harold, *The Relevance of British Socialism*, Weidenfeld & Nicolson (1964).

Unnamed Labour Party Publications
Annual Conference Reports.
A Guide for Women's Sections (March 1965).
HOW, WHEN & WHY? A Guide for Young Socialists (June 1966).
Party Organisation (1966) and (1975).

Unpublished Labour Party Documents
Report on the Working Party on Women's Organisation (May 1968). NAD/W/77/5/68.
Women and the Labour Party. "Statement by the National Labour Women's Advisory Council to the NEC." NAD/64/9/71 (R)
Women's Organisation within the Labour Party. "History & Background." NAD/W/1/1/68.

Index